The Crisis of Muslim History

Religion and Politics in Early Islam

RELATED TITLES PUBLISHED BY ONEWORLD

Al-Farabi: His Life, Works and Influence, Majid Fakhry, ISBN 1–85168–302–X
Approaches to Islam in Religious Studies, Richard C. Martin, ISBN 1–85168–268–6
As Through a Veil, Annemarie Schimmel, ISBN 1–85168–274–0
Averroes: His Life, Works and Influence, Majid Fakhry, ISBN 1–85168–269–4
A Concise Encyclopedia of Islam, Gordon D. Newby, ISBN 1–85168–295–3
The Faith and Practice of Al-Ghazálí, William Montgomery Watt, ISBN 1–85168–062–4
Faith and Reason in Islam, Averroes, translated with an introduction by Ibrahim Najjar, ISBN 1–85168–263–5
The Formative Period of Islamic Thought, William Montgomery Watt, ISBN 1–85168–152–3
Islam and the West, Norman Daniel, ISBN 1–85168–129–9
Islam: A Short History, William Montgomery Watt, ISBN 1–85168–205–8
Islamic Philosophy, Theology and Mysticism, Majid Fakhry, ISBN 1–85168–252–X
The Legacy of Arab–Islam in Africa, John Alembillah Azumah, ISBN 1–85168–273–2
The Mantle of the Prophet, Roy Mottahedeh, ISBN 1–85168–234–1
Muhammad: A Short Biography, Martin Forward, ISBN 1–85168–131–0
Muslim Women Mystics, Margaret Smith, ISBN 1–85168–250–3
On Being a Muslim, Farid Esack, ISBN 1–85168–146–9
Progressive Muslims: On Justice, Gender and Pluralism, edited by Omid Safi, ISBN 1–85168–316–X
The Qur'an and its Exegesis, Helmut Gätje, ISBN 1–85168–118–3
The Qur'an: A Short Introduction, Farid Esack, ISBN 1–85168–231–7
Qur'an, Liberation and Pluralism, Farid Esack, ISBN 1–85168–121–3
Revival and Reform in Islam, Fazlur Rahman, edited and with an introduction by Ebrahim Moosa, ISBN 1–85168–204–X
A Rumi Anthology, Reynold A. Nicholson, ISBN 1–85168–251–1
Rumi: Past and Present, East and West, Franklin D. Lewis, ISBN 1–85168–214–7
Speaking in God's Name: Islamic Law, Authority and Women, Khaled Abou El Fadl, ISBN 1–85168–262–7
Sufism: A Short Introduction, William C. Chittick, ISBN 1–85168–211–2
Tradition and Survival: A Bibliographical Survey of Early Shī'ite Literature, Hossein Modarressi, ISBN 1–85168–331–3
What Muslims Believe, John Bowker, ISBN 1–85168–169–8

The Crisis of Muslim History

Religion and Politics in Early Islam

Mahmoud M. Ayoub

ONEWORLD
OXFORD

THE CRISIS OF MUSLIM HISTORY

Oneworld Publications
(Sales and Editorial)
185 Banbury Road
Oxford OX2 7AR
England
www.oneworld-publications.com

A CIP record for this title is available
from the British Library

ISBN 1–85168–326–7

Cover design by Saxon Graphics, Derby UK
Typeset by Servis Filmsetting Ltd, Manchester, UK
Printed and bound in China by Sun Fung Offset Binding Co. Ltd

Contents

Preface

This monograph is the result of a larger research work, which is yet to be completed, dealing with the life and time of the Imām Ja'far al-Ṣādiq. The aim of both works is to study the interaction of religion with politics in early Islam. The present study, however, is limited to the period of the first four caliphs, which is believed by the majority of Muslims to represent the "Divinely Guided" caliphate.

The period of Prophetic rule in Madīnah belongs to sacred history. This is because, in the view of Muslims, it was guided not by human wisdom but Divine revelation, and hence can never be duplicated. Thus Muslim history, properly speaking, begins not with the career of the Prophet, nor even with his migration (*hijrah*), but with his death. It begins with the community's faltering steps towards building a concrete abode (*dār*) for Islam, whose foundations were laid by the Prophet and his intimate Companions. It begins with the rule of the four "Rightly Guided" caliphs, with which this study is concerned.

An adequate understanding of this formative period is crucial for our understanding of subsequent Islamic thought and history, yet it has been the subject of only a few specialized studies which are not readily accessible to the student of religion. The aim of this work therefore, is to fill this gap, not only for students of religion in general, but also for students of Islam. This small volume is intended to supplement the information usually presented in general introductions to Islam used by both graduate and undergraduate students in colleges and universities where English is the medium of instruction. A list of further readings in English translations of primary sources, when available, are referenced with the originals in the bibliography appended to this monograph.

This work was begun several years before the appearance of Professor Madelung's seminal book, *The Succession to Muḥammad: A Study of the Early Caliphate*, on the same subject. It is different in both scope and purpose. For, while Madelung's work ends with the consolidation of Umayyad power under the able Marwanid Caliph ʻAbd al-Malik b. Marwān (r. A.H. 65–86/684–705 C.E.), the present volume will conclude with the death of ʻAlī, the end of whose rule was coterminous with the period of the normative or "Rightly Guided" caliphate.

It remains for me to acknowledge with gratitude some of the organizations and people who helped in one way or another in the making of this study. My first indebtedness is to the Muhammadi Islamic Trust of Great Britain and its late director Commander Qasim Husayn who started me on this research venture. I am also indebted to the Iranian United Nations Mission, and particularly his Excellency, former Ambassador and present Foreign Minister Dr. Kamal Kharrazi for a generous grant which enabled me to complete the research for the book on the Imām al-Ṣādiq, on which this study is based. I am also grateful to Ms. Rose Ftaya for her patient and thorough editing of the book.

I undertook this work fully aware of the sensitivity of its subject and my own inadequacy for such a task. I have done my best to let the sources themselves tell the story of this crisis of Muslim history. This meant that little attention is paid to Western scholarship, not because I am not cognizant of the great contributions Western scholars have made to a better understanding of Islam and its civilization, but because I wish to let classical Muslim historians and traditionists give their own account of their own formative history. My intention is not to offend, defend, or apologize for anyone, any idea, legal school, or doctrine. My only hope is that this book will fulfill its stated purpose, which is to provide a useful introduction to the study of a crucial period of the history of Islam and its people.

Mahmoud M. Ayoub
Department of Religion
Temple University
Philadelphia

Rabīʿ al-Awwal, 1424 / May, 2003

1

Introduction

No, by God, be of good cheer, for God would never disgrace you! You surely treat your next-of-kin with kindness. You always speak the truth and endure weariness patiently. You receive the guest hospitably and lend assistance in times of adversity.[1]

Islam came into a society governed by moral principles based, not on faith in a sovereign God to whom all beings must answer on a day of judgment, but on time-honored customs which embodied certain values capable of holding society together and preserving its moral fabric. The words quoted above with which Khadījah, the Prophet's wife, sought to reassure him in his moment of deep spiritual and psychological crisis do not invoke religious piety or right belief, but moral values of kindness, patience, hospitality, and reliability. Islam affirmed these values, gave them a broader moral framework of social responsibility, and deepened their religious meaning. It enjoined kindness not only to one's next-of-kin but to the orphan, the needy, and the wayfarer. It called for patience and steadfastness not only in times of misfortune, but also in resisting oppression and wrongdoing whenever it might be found. Through obligatory alms (*zakāt*) Islam

1. Abū al-Fidā' Ismā'īl Ibn Kathīr, *Tafsīr al-Qur'ān al-'aẓīm*, 2nd edn., 7 vols. (Beirut: Dār al-Fikr, 1389/1970), vol. 7, pp. 325–326.

made social responsibility a religious duty and an act of worship and purification.

Muḥammad ruled the first Muslim commonwealth – which he founded in 622, twelve years after his prophetic call – primarily as a prophet. His role as a statesman was only a means of realizing a socio-political order based on a revealed law (*sharīʿah*). To this end, he struggled for a base of operation until he secured a safehaven in Madīnah. From that secure base the Prophet, his fellow Immigrants (*muhājirūn*), and Supporters (*anṣār*) waged a continuous battle against his own recalcitrant people for the spread of the new faith with its community and power. That being the ultimate objective, all hostilities were forgotten as soon as the goal was achieved. The Prophet's aim was to establish a faith-community rather than an empire. He died, therefore, without leaving a clear and concrete political model or apparatus that could sustain the vast empire which arose with amazing rapidity following his death.

The two primary frameworks within which the Islamic social order was constructed were the life-example (*sunnah*) of the Prophet Muḥammad, and the Qur'ān. Apart from actions relating to daily prayers and other ritualistic matters, the Prophetic *sunnah* consists largely of moral directives with occasional illustrative or supportive anecdotes. There is little in the *sunnah* that can serve as the basis for a political system as we understand it today. There are, to be sure, numerous *ḥadīth* traditions with clear political purport. Such traditions, however, reflect not what the Prophet may have said or done, but the political crises, views, and ideals of later generations.[2] As for the Qur'ān, like any sacred scripture it is open to endless interpretation as demanded by changing circumstances. This infinite possibility of meaning and interpretation is attested in the Qur'ān itself, which declares: "No one knows its interpretation [*ta'wīl*] except God" (Q.3:7).[3] Moreover, before the

2. For a brief but illuminating discussion of this issue, see Fred M. Donner, *Narratives of Islamic Origins. The Beginnings of Islamic Historical Writing* (Princeton: Darwin Press, 1998), pp. 40–47.
3. For various interpretations of this controversial verse see M. Ayoub, *The Qur'ān and*

legal principles of the Qur'ān and *sunnah* could be fully implemented they had to be codified into a complex system of law. This process lagged far behind the social and political exigencies the law was meant to cover. In fact, neither the Qur'ān nor the Prophetic tradition provides a clear political direction for the community.

The Shī'ī doctrine of the imamate is an example of an early attempt to formulate a political structure within a juridical framework and does, indeed, present a coherent political theory. However, the basic principle of succession which this doctrine propounds was never universally accepted and has remained an unrealized eschatological hope. Some of the difficulties of interpreting and translating the Prophetic *sunnah* into political theory are demonstrated in the history of the tradition that underlies the doctrine.

The doctrine was, according to Shī'ī tradition, enunciated in principle by the Prophet after his Farewell Pilgrimage at Ghadīr Khumm, a spot between Makkah and Madīnah. The *ḥadīth* of al-Ghadīr, which proclaims 'Alī to be the rightful successor (*khalīfah*) of Muḥammad, exists in many and widely divergent recensions and has been the subject of much debate and controversy in Muslim theology, historiography, jurisprudence, and political theory.[4] Significantly, although this Prophetic *ḥadīth* is regarded by Shī'ī tradition as the decisive proof-text (*naṣṣ*) of 'Alī's designation as the imām of the Muslims after Muḥammad, 'Alī is nowhere reported to have invoked it in support of his right to the caliphate in his debate with Abū Bakr and 'Umar. But this does not obviate the fact that Shī'ī *ḥadīth* and theological sources present this tradition as an incontrovertible argument in support of 'Alī's right to succeed Muḥammad as leader of the Muslim *ummah*. I shall return to this important tradition when we consider 'Alī's struggle to assert his right to the caliphate, his turbulent rule, and its tragic end.

its Interpreters, 2 vols. (Albany: State University of New York Press, 1992), vol. 2, pp. 20–46.

4. For a comprehensive discussion of the al-Ghadīr tradition from a Shī'ī point of view, see 'Abd al-Ḥusayn Aḥmad al-Amīnī, *al-Ghadīr fī al-kitāb wal-sunnah wal-adab*, 4th edn., 11 vols. (Beirut: Dār al-Kitāb al-'Arabī, 1397/1977), esp. vols. 1 and 2.

This monograph is a spin-off of a much larger work on the life and times of the sixth Shīʿī Imām, Jaʿfar al-Ṣādiq, which was begun over a decade ago, and which still awaits completion. The purpose of the present study is to fill an important gap that is manifest in most general introductions to Islam – there is a need for a clear and somewhat comprehensive presentation of the formative period of Muslim history following the death of the Prophet Muḥammad. The present volume is meant to help redress this problem and thus provide the background necessary for a better understanding of subsequent developments in Islamic thought and history.

In this study I shall briefly examine the political and socio-religious crisis of early Muslim history, and reflect on the changing perceptions and applications of old Arab customs and values in their Islamic context. To achieve this goal, I shall let the primary sources of Muslim thought and history themselves tell the story of the crisis and its effects.

These important historical and literary narratives were written by men who were themselves deeply engaged in the centuries-long debates surrounding this crisis and its aftermath. Their narratives therefore provide us with the best context for our study of the early unfolding of Muslim history from the vantage of Muslim historiography. While the actual events surrounding this crisis were soon shrouded with thick layers of myth, legend, and ideological considerations, the diversity of sources here employed will itself, I hope, allow us to investigate them with a good measure of credibility. I have not, however, used the sources uncritically; they have been carefully chosen to represent the wide diversity of Muslim perspectives. This approach may be new to Western scholarship, but I feel it has its value. I trust that this methodology will help us see in clearer perspective the profound and far-reaching effect this crisis has left on the Muslim community.

Two primary considerations have led me to concentrate on the period of the first four caliphs. The first is that these men are regarded by the majority of Muslims as true heirs to the Prophet in their piety, courage, justice, and wisdom. They were ideal rulers, collectively called *al-khulafā' al-rāshidūn* (the rightly guided caliphs). Hence, the rule of Abū Bakr, 'Umar, 'Uthmān, and 'Alī is considered by all Sunni Muslims to be the normative period of Muslim history. In contrast, Shī'ī Muslims have condemned the rule of the first three caliphs as one of usurpation of 'Alī's sole right to the caliphate.

Western scholars have, not without justification, considered this period an era of violent struggle for power, resulting in a long period of protracted civil strife.[5] It must be observed in this connection that the rule of all four caliphs was characterized by dissension and conflict, and all except Abū Bakr died violent deaths. The history is so evocative that both Muslim and Western scholars have felt compelled to take strong political and moral positions on the side of this or that party to the conflict. Not until the publication of Wilfred Madelung's important work on the period, do we have a conscious attempt to "let the sources speak for themselves."[6]

The second consideration is the crucial role this brief but turbulent period has played in the development of Islamic religious and political thought, including the rise of theological and legal schools. Subsequent to the tragic caliphate of 'Alī and his equally tragic death, the four major divisions in the Muslim *ummah* appeared. These were the *shī'ah*, or party of 'Alī; the *khawārij*, or seceders, who deserted 'Alī and regarded any authority in the *ummah* other than their own to be illegitimate, and therefore to be destroyed; the *mu'tazilah*, who isolated themselves from political life altogether;[7] and the *murji'ah*, who

5. See, for a good representative of this view, Julius Wellhausen, *The Arab Kingdom and its Fall*, trans. Margaret Graham Weir (Calcutta: University of Calcutta, 1927).
6. Wilfred Madelung, *The Succession to Muḥammad: A Study of the Early Caliphate* (Cambridge: Cambridge University Press, 1997). The author claims to have inherited this virtue from his mother "who taught him to see history as it really is," as he asserts in his dedication of the book to her.
7. A socio-political phenomenon in Muslim history, which appeared during the caliphate of 'Alī, as we shall see below. The theological school, which emerged about half a century later under the same name, inherited both the designation and political neutrality of this original phenomenon.

withheld judgment regarding the ultimate fate of all parties to the conflict that led to ʿAlī's assassination – and hence of grave sinners in general – leaving it to God Himself to judge on the day of the final reckoning. Although the ideological and theological movements that took on these designations developed later, their roots clearly go back to the issues and attitudes which had divided the Muslim community during this early period of its history.

For centuries these four movements represented the major trends in Muslim theological, philosophical, and political thought. Their influence, moreover, may be discerned to this day in the sectarian factions which continue to divide what was meant to be a single and unified *ummah*, as clearly envisioned by the Qur'ān: "This *ummah* of yours is one *ummah* and I am your Lord, so worship me"(Q.21:92).[8]

8. It may in fact be argued on the basis of this important verse that the principle of the unity of the Islamic *ummah* is rooted in the Qu'rānic doctrine of Divine Oneness (*tawḥīd*).

2

The Crisis of Succession

The death of the Prophet Muḥammad in 632 after a ten-year rule over the nascent Muslim community was a shock the effects of which have dominated Islamic history. It precipitated a religious as well as political crisis, and left a power vacuum which had to be filled if the new community and its faith were not to disintegrate and collapse. That this would have happened is clear from the fact that, immediately after his accession to the caliphate, Abū Bakr had to wage bloody wars against neighboring tribes that sought either to secede from the new Islamic order or to present rival claimants to Muḥammad's prophetic authority. Unfortunately, the accounts that classical historians preserved of this great crisis and its resolution were written long after the events. They are thus colored by later circumstances and the religio-political ideas and attitudes they engendered. These accounts are nonetheless valuable for our purpose because they contain material that reflects the attitudes and perceptions that motivated early Muslim society and its makers.

Classical sources reveal that several important factors were considered in deciding the question of succession to the Prophet's leadership of the community. These were, first, blood or tribal relationship to Muḥammad; second, priority in entering into Islam, and hence the length of the period of companionship (*ṣuḥbah*) with the Prophet; and finally, social status. It is noteworthy that none of these considerations is purely religious. Questions of personal piety and moral integrity may not have been pertinent in the case of the pious close Companions of the Prophet. However, the arguments that Abū Bakr and 'Umar advanced in support of the exclusive right of the men of the Quraysh to the caliphate, in the first public debate of the issue, set the tone for all subsequent claims to this high office. It is therefore necessary to treat this crucial debate in some detail, and closely analyze its various elements and implications.

The Saqīfah Debate and its Aftermath

An early account of this debate is preserved in the history of the caliphate attributed to 'Abd Allāh b. Muslim b. Qutaybah al-Dīnawarī (d. 276/889). Ibn Qutaybah reports that al-'Abbās, the Prophet's uncle, met 'Alī ibn Abī Ṭālib as the Prophet lay dying and said:

> The Prophet is about to die! Go, therefore, and ask him if this affair [that is the caliphate] shall be ours, that he may declare it. But if it belongs to someone else, then he may at least enjoin kindness towards us.

Al-'Abbās then went to Abū Bakr and 'Umar and asked if the Prophet had left any instructions concerning the matter; both concurred that he had said nothing. Immediately after the Prophet died, al-'Abbās returned and said to 'Alī:

> Stretch out your hand that I may pledge allegiance (*bay'ah*) to you, for then people would say, "The uncle of the Messenger of God pledged allegiance to the cousin of the Messenger of God." Your own relatives will then offer their *bay'ah* and all the people will follow suit.

'Alī asked, "Will anyone quarrel with us concerning this matter?"[1]

This account clearly supports the view that the Prophet died

1. 'Abd Allāh b. Muslim b. Qutaybah (*pseudo*), *al-Imāmah wal-siyāsah aw ta'rīkh al-khulafā'*, ed. 'Alī Shīrī, 2 vols. (Beirut: Dār al-Aḍwā', 1410/1990), vol. 1, p. 21. This important work was probably written in Islamic Spain in the tenth century and falsely attributed to Ibn Qutaybah. See the editor's introduction. The famous historian 'Alī b. Aḥmad al-Maqrīzī relates several versions of this report in his book *Kitāb al-Nizā' wa-al-takhāṣum fīmā bayn banī Umayya wa-banī Hāshim* (Leiden: E. J. Brill, 1888), pp. 34–36.

without appointing anyone to succeed him. There seems to be no doubt that, as we shall see presently, the Anṣār of Madīnah ultimately preferred 'Alī to all the Muhājirūn of the Quraysh. Yet, had they understood the words of the Prophet at Ghadīr Khumm "Anyone whose master (*mawlā*) I am, 'Alī also is his master" to imply caliphal authority, it is unlikely that they would have met to choose one from among themselves for that office.[2] They only seemed to favor 'Alī's appointment when their own claim to the caliphate was irrevocably thwarted. Moreover, when they as well as other prominent Companions championed 'Alī's cause, they appear to have been motivated not by a clear and direct prophetic declaration (*naṣṣ*) of 'Alī's appointment, but by 'Alī's personal qualities of courage, wisdom, piety, sound judgment, and profound religious knowledge and insight. 'Alī's close kinship to the Prophet, and hence his right to the inheritance of the Prophet's authority, was certainly also a crucial factor in 'Alī's favor.[3]

Be that as it may, Ibn Qutaybah reports, on the authority of 'Abd Allāh b. 'Abd al-Raḥmān al-Anṣārī, that when the rumour of the Prophet's death was spread among the people, the Anṣār gathered at the *saqīfah*[4] of the tribe of the Banū Sā'idah around Sa'd b. 'Ubādah, a notable of the Anṣār of the Khazraj tribe. Sa'd was at the time ill and unable to stand up. Still, he spoke at length of the many excellences of the Anṣār, their priority in accepting Islam, and their support of the Prophet. He then counselled his people saying, "Strengthen your hold on this affair, for you have the most rightful claim to it, and you are the most worthy of men of it."[5]

2. Indeed, Madelung's suggestion that the Anṣār initially met to choose a chief (*amīr*) for themselves rather than a leader for the Muslim community at large, is plausible as the caliphal office had as yet not been instituted, let alone clearly thought out. Madelung, pp. 30 ff.
3. For a comprehensive account of this debate underscoring 'Alī's right to the caliphate, see Ibn Abī al-Ḥadīd, *Sharḥ nahj al-balāghah*, ed. Muḥammad Abū al-Fadl Ibrahīm, 3rd edn., 20 vols. (Beirut: Dār al-Fikr, 1399/1979), vol. 2, pp. 21–26; vol. 6, pp. 5–49.
4. A *saqīfah* is an open, loosely roofed, meeting place.
5. Ibn Qutaybah, vol. 1, p. 22.

News of this gathering soon reached Abū Bakr and 'Umar who quickly hastened to the *saqīfah*, accompanied by Abū 'Ubaydah b. al-Jarrāḥ. Abū Bakr argued for the right of the Muhājirūn to the leadership (*imārah*) of the Muslims after the death of their Prophet on the basis of the Muhājirūn's priority in entering into Islam and their noble lineage among the Arabs. He admitted the special status of the Anṣār in the Muslim community and continued, "You are our assistants [*wuzarā'*] in the affairs of religion and the Supporters of the Messenger of God. You are our brothers in upholding the Book of God and our partners in the Religion of God."[6]

Abū Bakr then counselled the Anṣār of Madīnah not to be jealous of their brothers, the Muhājirūn of the Quraysh, for they alone had the right to the caliphal office. He then suggested that the Supporters choose either Abū 'Ubaydah or 'Umar. Both of these men, however, declined the honor. They deferred to Abū Bakr whom they considered to be more worthy of succession to the Prophet on account of his age and priority in Islam. Additional justifications included the fact that Abū Bakr was alone with the Prophet in the cave (*'al-Ghār'*) during their flight from Makkah to Madīnah (Q.9:40) and the report that the Prophet had entrusted Abū Bakr to lead the prayers during his last illness, both of which gave him priority over other Companions. These arguments are undoubtedly late. They reflect subsequent Shī'ī–Sunni polemics rather than the opinions of the contenders in this early caliphal debate.

The men of the Anṣār assured Abū Bakr and his two companions that they were not envious of them, and that they held them in high esteem. But, they continued:

> We fear what tomorrow may bring. We are afraid that someone who is from among neither us nor you may seize this office. If you were today to appoint one man of us and one of you, we would certainly give allegiance and agree that when he dies, a man of the Anṣār would succeed him. When this man dies he would likewise be succeeded by a man of the Muhājirūn and so on, so long as this community endures.

6. Ibid., p. 23.

In this way, the Anṣār argued, justice would be maintained. Thus if the man of the Quraysh appeared to deviate from the right course, the Anṣār would restrain him, and vice versa. Abū Bakr, however, held his ground and insisted:

> The Muhājirūn are the first people on earth to worship God truly, and the first to accept faith in God and His Messenger. They are, moreover, Muḥammad's heirs (*awlīyā'*) and kinsmen (*'ashīrah*), and therefore most deserving of this office after him. No man would dispute their right to it except a wrongdoer. We are therefore the chiefs (*umarā'*) and you are the subordinates (*wuzarā'*). We shall not agree to any consultation without you, nor shall any matter be decided without your consent.[7]

Here, Ibn Qutaybah's account presents the conflict between the Quraysh of Makkah and the Anṣār of Madīnah as one of political authority and economic power. The point is clearly brought out in an argument ascribed to Ḥubāb b. al-Mundhir of the Aws tribe. Ḥubāb began by arguing that the Immigrants had, in fact, no right or priority over the Supporters. This, because God was not worshiped openly except in the land of the Anṣār, congregational prayers were not offered except in their mosques, nor were the Arabs subdued except by their swords. He concluded, "If the people will not agree, then let us all choose an *amīr* first from among us, who will be succeeded by an *amīr* from among them." 'Umar countered this suggestion with the argument that "The caliphate can only belong to a people if they also possess the office of prophethood, and it is they [the Quraysh] who are the people of Muḥammad."[8]

Abū Bakr finally clinched the argument by reminding the Anṣār of their own old and bloody hostilities:

> If the men of the Khazraj were to show their ambition concerning this affair, the men of the Aws would not fall far behind. Likewise, were the men of the Aws to seek it, those of the Khazraj would surely do the same. There are, moreover, between these two tribes deaths and injuries that can never be healed. If therefore any man of either of you were to bellow

7. Ibid., p. 24.
8. Ibid., pp. 24–25.

> out his claim to this office, he would place himself between the two jaws of a lion: to be chewed up by his Qurayshite opponent, or wounded by his rival of the Anṣār.[9]

Abū Bakr succeeded in rekindling the old mistrust between the two Madinan tribes which Islam had sought to alleviate,[10] and quickly divided the men in the *saqīfah* into two opposing camps.

Soon the Anṣār disagreed as to whether the first caliph ought to be of the Aws or Khazraj. After much bickering one of the notables of the Aws, Bashīr b. S'ad, broke ranks with the Supporters and sided with the Immigrants. As most of the men present rushed to pledge allegiance to Abū Bakr, a state of general confusion ensued. Seeing this, Ḥubāb exclaimed, "So you have done it, O men of the Anṣār! By God, I can see your sons standing at their doors begging with outstretched hands, but they are not even given water to drink!" "Are you afraid of us, O Ḥubāb?" Abū Bakr asked. Ḥubāb replied, "It is not of you that I am afraid, but of whoever comes after you." Abū Bakr retorted:

> If it ever comes to that, then you and your people should take matters into your own hands. You will be under no obligation to obey us in anything.[11]

The second of our sources, Abū Muḥammad Aḥmad b. A'tham al-Kūfī (d. *c.* 314/926) begins his narrative neither with al-'Abbās and 'Alī nor with the Saqīfah Debate, but with Abū Bakr's famous declaration announcing the Prophet's death: "Let anyone who worshiped Muḥammad know that Muḥammad is dead! But as for those who worship God, He is Everliving and shall never die." Abū Bakr then addressed the men gathered at the Prophet's Mosque:

9. 'Uthmān b. Baḥr al-Jāḥiẓ, *al-Bayān wal-tabyīn*, ed. Ḥasan Sandūbī, 3 vols. (Cairo: Maṭba'at al-Istiqāmah, 1366/1947), vol. 3, pp. 250–251. For a contemporary Shi'ī discussion of Abū Bakr's role in the Saqīfah Debate, see Muḥammad Mahdī Shams al-Dīn, *Niẓām al-ḥukm wal-idārah fī al-islām*, 4th edn. (Beirut: al-Mu'assassah al-duwaliyyah lil-dirāsah wal-nashr, 1415/1995), pp. 57–62.
10. See Jawād 'Alī, *al-Mufaṣṣal fī tarīkh al-'arab qabl al-islām*, 3rd edn., 10 vols. (Beirut: Dār al-'ilm lil-malāyīn, 1970–80), vol. 4 (1980), pp. 137–140.
11. Ibn Qutaybah, vol. 1, pp. 26–27.

> Muḥammad has passed away and it is imperative that a man be set up in authority to take charge of this affair. Ponder the matter therefore, consider it carefully and give your opinion. May God have mercy upon you.[12]

This account is especially significant for two reasons. It assigns a direct and unquestionable leadership role to Abū Bakr, which naturally supports his claim to the caliphate; and consequently, it implicitly renders the Saqīfah event virtually insignificant. In fact, this historian negates the Saqīfah meeting altogether by making Abū Bakr preside over his own election to the caliphal office – and, not before a small and disparate group of men in the *saqīfah* of the Banū Sā'idah, but in the Prophet's Mosque and before all the Muslims. After this initial but conclusive report, Ibn A'tham goes on to briefly recount the Saqīfah Debate.

Having ascertained the death of the Prophet, Ibn A'tham reports, the men of the Anṣār gathered in the *saqīfah* of the Banū Sā'idah to choose a man from amongst themselves. He relates that it was Khuzaymah b. Thābit, a well-known man of the Anṣār whose testimony the Prophet declared to be equal to that of two men, who championed the cause of the Anṣār. Usayd b. Ḥuḍayr, another notable of the Anṣār whom the Prophet had chosen as one of the twelve men to be his special deputies (*nuqabā'*) in Madīnah, led the opposition. Here again we see that opposition was based not on considerations of religious piety or political acumen but rather on tribal affiliation. Usayd and his fellows opposed the nomination of Sa'd b. 'Ubādah because he was of the Khazraj and they were of the Aws tribe. Speaking for the opposition 'Uwaym b. Sā'idah, another notable of the Anṣār, argued:

> O men of the Anṣār, you were the first to fight in defense of this religion; be not the first to fight its people for authority over it! The caliphate can belong only to the people of prophethood. Place it, therefore, where God

12. Abū Muḥammad Aḥmad b. A'tham al-Kūfī, *Kitāb al-futūḥ*, 1st edn., 8 vols. (Ḥaydarabād: Wizārat al-Ma'ārif al-Hind, n.d. [Repr. Beirut: Dār al-Nadwah al-Jadīdah, n.d.]), vol. 1, pp. 2–3. It should be noted that both the death date and the work of Ibn A'tham al Kūfī have been the subject of controversy.

> had placed it, for the people of Quraysh are favored with the prayer of Abraham.[13]

In Ibn A'tham's report then, not only is the debate insignificant, but the role of Abū Bakr as instigator of the rift between the Anṣār of the Khazraj and the Aws is completely absent. Moreover, while stressing the internal division between the two Anṣār tribes, he gives the support, which the Anṣār extend for the right of Quraysh to the caliphate, scriptural authority.

The famous historian al-Ya'qūbī (d. *c.* 900) adds few, but significant details to the account of the debate. He reports that Abū Bakr said to the Anṣār, when proposing 'Umar or Abū 'Ubaydah for the caliphate, "This is 'Umar b. al-Khaṭṭāb concerning whom the Messenger of God prayed, 'O God, strengthen this religion with 'Umar!' Here is also Abū 'Ubaydah b. al-Jarrāḥ, of whom the Messenger of God said, 'He is the trustful man [*amīn*] of this community.'"[14]

Ya'qūbī includes another man in the disputation. He is 'Abd al-Raḥmān b. 'Awf who, as we shall see, was to play a pivotal role in the second crisis of caliphal succession. According to Ya'qūbī, 'Abd al-Raḥmān argued, "O men of the Anṣār, although you are people of great virtue, there are no men among you like Abū Bakr, 'Umar or 'Alī." Al-Mundhir b. Arqam, a well-known Companion of the Anṣār, replied, "We do not deny the excellence of the men you mention. There is among them one with whom no one would dispute if he were to claim this office." Ya'qūbī comments that al-Mundhir meant 'Alī b. Abī Ṭālib.[15]

Ya'qūbī finally reports that, as men rushed to pledge allegiance to

13. Ibid., p. 4. For the prayer of Abraham see Q.14:37, which reads: "My Lord, I have made part of my progeny to dwell in an uncultivable valley near Your sacred house in order, Our Lord, that they establish regular prayers. Our Lord, make therefore the hearts of men to incline towards them and provide them with diverse fruits; perhaps they will give thanks." See also, Q.2:127–129.
14. Aḥmad b. Abū Ya'qūb b. Ja'far b. Wahb b. Wāḍiḥ al-Ya'qūbī, *Ta'rīkh al-Ya'qūbī*, 2 vols. (Beirut: Dār Ṣādir, n.d.), vol. 2, p. 123.
15. Ibid.

Abū Bakr they nearly trampled Sa'd b. 'Ubādah. 'Umar exclaimed, "Kill Sa'd, may God kill Sa'd!"[16] Sa'd was in fact later mysteriously killed in Syria where he lived in a self-imposed exile, perhaps at the instigation of 'Umar.[17]

Muḥammad b. Jarīr al-Ṭabarī (d. 310/923) presents by far the fullest account of the Saqīfah event. He presents two different, but highly interesting reports. The first, related on the authority of Ibn 'Abbās who heard it from 'Abd al-Raḥmān b. 'Awf, demonstrates clearly 'Umar's doubt concerning the legitimacy of the procedure by which Abū Bakr was brought to power, and the political motive behind his election. The second report, related on the authority of the well-known but controversial Shī'ī traditionist Abū Mikhnaf, focuses on the question of the exclusive right of the Quraysh to the caliphate. These are issues that have occupied Muslim historians, theologians, and jurists ever since.

First, Ṭabarī reports that, while 'Umar was away on the *ḥajj* pilgrimage, 'Abd al-Raḥmān b. 'Awf heard a man say, "Were the Commander of the Faithful to die, I would pledge allegiance to so and so."[18] When 'Umar returned and heard what the man had said, he declared, "Let no man be deceived into thinking that Abū Bakr's *bay'ah* was not a slip! Indeed it was, but God has averted its evil." 'Umar then went on to justify Abū Bakr's *bay'ah* not on the grounds of its legitimacy, but on the basis of the latter's piety and social standing.[19]

Having thus justified Abū Bakr's *bay'ah*, 'Umar related what had happened at the *saqīfah* of the Banū Sā'idah. Abū Bakr, we are told,

16. Ibid., p. 124.
17. Sa'd is reported to have been killed by the *jinn* who boasted: "We have surely killed Sa'd b. 'Ubādah; we shot him with two arrows and did not miss his heart." See 'Izz al-Dīn Ibn al-Athīr Abū al-Ḥasan 'Alī b. Muḥammad al-Jazarī, *Usd al ghābah fī ma'rifat al-ṣaḥābah*, 1st edn., 8 vols. (Beirut: Dār al-kutub al-'ilmiyyah, 1414/1996), vol. 2, pp. 441–443.
18. Ibn Abī al-Ḥadīd (vol. 2, pp. 25–26) reports that this man was 'Ammār b. Yāsir who intended 'Alī. According to another report, it was Ṭalḥah b. 'Ubayd Allāh.
19. For different interpretations of this enigmatic statement and its justification, see ibid., pp. 26–39.

argued the case of the Quraysh on the grounds of their noble lineage. ʿUmar further argued in defense of the manner of securing Abū Bakr's *bayʿah*:

> By God, there was nothing we could do better at that time than to give *bayʿah* to Abū Bakr. We feared that if we had left the people without concluding a *bayʿah*, they would have done so on their own. Then we would have had to either agree to something we did not like, or risk dissension.[20]

In his second account, Ṭabarī relates on the authority of Abū Mikhnaf that Abū Bakr was in the Prophet's house when the latter died. This is important because it runs counter to the common Shīʿī belief that ʿAlī alone was with the Prophet at that time. As ʿAlī was busy preparing the Prophet's body for burial, ʿUmar, according to this account, came in and urged Abū Bakr to go with him to the *saqīfah* of the Banū Sāʿidah. The two men, accompanied by Abū ʿUbaydah b. al-Jarrāḥ, hurried there.

As they arrived, the men of the Anṣār were hotly debating the issue of succession. When the suggestion was made that the office of the caliphate be held successively by men of the Anṣār and the Quraysh, Saʿd b. ʿUbādah exclaimed, "This, by God, is the beginning of weakness!" Abū Bakr, as we have seen, rejected the suggestion with his famous assertion, "We are the chiefs (*umarāʾ*) and you are the subordinates (*wuzarāʾ*)." Ṭabarī presents a telling retort in which Ḥubāb b. al-Mundhir countered Abū Bakr's claim saying:

> O men of the Anṣār, take full control of your affairs! No man will ever dare oppose you, and all the people will submit to your opinion. You are the people of honor and wealth. You are the people of great multitudes and strength. You are the people of experience and prowess and of help in times of trouble. All the people are watching carefully what you do. Do not, therefore, be divided lest your opinion lose its authority and your resolve collapse.

20. Muḥammad ibn Jarīr al-Ṭabarī, *Taʾrīkh al-rusul wa-al-mulūk*, ed. Muḥammad Abū al-Faḍl Ibrahīm, 4th edn., 13 vols. (Cairo: Dār al-Maʿārif, 1382/1962), vol. 3, pp. 203–206. This account is also reported in Bukhārī, see *Ṣaḥīḥ al-bukhārī* (*K. al-Ḥudūd*, *ḥadīth* 6328).

Ḥubāb then proposed that the principle of succession that the men of the Anṣār championed be achieved by force if necessary. 'Umar, however, insisted:

> Alas, no two men can hold equal power together. By God, the Arabs would never agree to set you in authority over them when their Prophet is of another people. But they would not refuse to delegate the management of their affairs to those among whom prophethood appeared [that is the Quraysh].[21]

It is significant that Ṭabarī here presents the Muhājirūn as advancing the same religious and genealogical arguments that 'Alī and other Hashimites have advanced ever since in support of their own claim to both spiritual and temporal authority in the Muslim community. The thrust of the arguments of both parties in the Saqīfah Debate was social prestige and political power. As we shall see presently, the proof of 'Alī's right to the caliphate rested on his Hashimite lineage, and hence his blood relationship to the Prophet, as well as on his priority (*sābiqah*) in accepting Islam. Yet he was consciously passed over, and neither he nor anyone of the notables of the house of Hāshim were even consulted in this most consequential matter.

Historians are agreed that 'Alī opposed the Saqīfah decision, and consequently, that he was coerced into giving allegiance to Abū Bakr. Most of them, however, have consciously tried to minimize the significance of his dissent. It is surprising that Ibn Qutaybah, or his actual author (a Sunni historian writing either in Umayyad Spain, or at a time when the 'Abbasid rulers had adopted Sunni orthodoxy as the framework of their authority), presents the struggle between 'Alī and the caliphal establishment more sharply and openly than most other historians, even those who are known to have clear Shī'ī sympathies. Ibn Qutaybah reports that while most of the Muhājirūn and Anṣār soon pledged allegiance to Abū Bakr, al-Zubayr (a well-known Companion and cousin of the Prophet) and the men of the Banū Hāshim withheld

21. al-Ṭabarī, vol. 3, pp. 218–220.

their *bay'ah* until they were compelled to offer it. When 'Alī was brought before Abū Bakr, he protested:

> I am the servant of God and the brother of the Messenger of God. I am thus more worthy of this office than you. I shall not give allegiance to you [meaning Abū Bakr and 'Umar] when it is more proper for you to give *bay'ah* to me. You have seized this office from the Anṣār using your tribal relationship to the Prophet as an argument against them. Would you then seize this office from us, the *ahl al-bayt*, [people of the house of the Prophet] by force? Did you not claim before the Anṣār that you were more worthy than they of the caliphate because Muḥammad came from among you – and thus they gave you the leadership and surrendered command? I now contend against you with the same argument with which you contended against the Anṣār. It is we who are more worthy of the Messenger of God, living or dead. Give us our due right if you truly have faith in God, or else bear the charge of wilfully doing wrong.

'Umar answered, "We will not leave you until you pledge allegiance!" 'Alī countered, "Has Abū Bakr plotted something in which you also have a part? You support him today in his scheme, and he will repay you tomorrow!" Abū 'Ubaydah then tried to convince 'Alī to acquiesce to the choice of Abū Bakr on the grounds that he, 'Alī, was too young for such a venerable office. But 'Alī insisted:

> O men of the Muhājirūn, do not remove Muḥammad's inheritance among the Arabs from his house to your own. Do not dislodge his own family members from his station and rights among the people. By God, we are more worthy of this office than you so long as there is one among us who is truly a reciter of the Book of God and a savant [*faqīh*] of the religion of God; who knows well the customs and laws [*sunan*] of the Messenger of God; who is well informed of the affairs of the people and is their protector against evil things; and who distributes wealth among them with equity. By God, such a man is one of us.[22]

We have quoted this statement extensively because it expresses well one of the two main components of the Shī'ī argument for 'Alī's right to the caliphate, namely his right to the inheritance of the Prophet's authority as his vicegerent (*waṣī*). The Shī'ī doctrine of the

22. Ibn Qutaybah, vol. 1, p. 29.

imamate is based on the principle of the vicegerency of a series of successors to one prophet until the coming of the next. As the last prophet, Muḥammad was heir to the knowledge and authority of all the prophets before him. According to this doctrine he bequeathed his knowledge and authority to ʻAlī as his first vicegerent. We shall return to the other major component of the doctrine, the Prophet's designation (*naṣṣ*) of ʻAlī as his successor (*khalīfah*) and imām of the Muslims, later. Suffice it to say here, that the statement just quoted presents all the prerequisites for a just and rightful imām from the point of view of Shīʻī theology and jurisprudence. These are membership in the Prophet's family (*ahl al-bayt*), piety, knowledge of the Qur'ān and the *sunnah* of the Prophet, concern for the welfare of the people, and justice in managing their affairs. That Ibn Qutaybah presents these points indicates clearly the tension in the Muslim community between piety and politics. Here Ibn Qutaybah portrays the ʻAlī of piety: pious, brave, learned. However, soon (and, as we shall see, in the same breath) he will present the ʻAlī of politics who is made to contradict his earlier argument for his claim to the caliphate.

Ibn Qutaybah reports that ʻAlī took Fāṭimah (his wife and the daughter of the Prophet), by night, to the assemblies of the Anṣār, calling on their support in his disagreement with his opponents of the Quraysh. He was told that, had he preceded Abū Bakr to the *saqīfah*, they would have certainly pledged allegiance to him. He argued, "Should I have left the Messenger of God in his house unburied and gone out to quarrel with men over his authority?" Fāṭimah added, "Abū al-Ḥasan [ʻAlī] did only what he should have done. But God will bring them [that is Abū Bakr and ʻUmar] to account for what they did."[23]

ʻAlī then decided to withhold allegiance from Abū Bakr. He withdrew with al-Zubayr and the men of Banū Hāshim to Fāṭimah's house. ʻUmar followed and threatened to set the house on fire if the people refused to come out and pledge allegiance. They all did, except ʻAlī.

23. Ibid., pp. 29–30.

'Umar asked Abū Bakr, "Will you not force this recalcitrant man to give *bay'ah*?" Abū Bakr, however, did not wish to compel 'Alī. Rather he sent his servant to him with the message "The successor (*khalīfah*) of the Messenger of God wishes to see you." 'Alī answered, "How soon you have uttered falsehood against the Messenger of God!" Hearing this, Abū Bakr wept. 'Umar himself then went and brought 'Alī out by force. 'Alī challenged 'Umar saying, "What if I do not give allegiance?" 'Umar answered, "We would cut off your head!" 'Alī retorted, "You would then have killed the brother of the Messenger of God!" 'Umar objected, "That you are the servant of God (*'abd Allāh*), yes, we agree, but that you are the brother of the Messenger of God, no, we do not."[24] 'Alī we are told, and with him all the sons of Hāshim, gave their allegiance to Abū Bakr only after Fāṭimah's death, although historians are not agreed on the exact time.

Ibn Qutaybah tempers this boisterous encounter between 'Alī and Abū Bakr and 'Umar with the following irenic account in which 'Alī's support of Abū Bakr's leadership is clearly stated. Once Abū Bakr had secured the allegiance of all the people, he spent three days in offering to release anyone who wished from allegiance to him, and himself asking to be excused from the onerous responsibility of leadership. He repeated, "You are all released from allegiance to me. Is there anyone who feels compelled? Is there anyone who is resentful?" But 'Alī arose before all the people present in the Prophet's Mosque and declared:

> By God, we shall never excuse you, or be released from our allegiance to you. The Messenger of God himself brought you to the fore [that is to lead the prayers during the Prophet's final illness] in order to unite us in our religion. Who would then dare remove you from the task of managing our worldly affairs.[25]

In another twist, Ya'qūbī reports that the men of Banū Hāshim were surprised to hear of Abū Bakr's election. This was because, as he observes, "Neither the Muhājirūn nor the Anṣār had any doubt regard-

24. Ibid., pp. 30–31.
25. Ibid., p. 33.

ing 'Alī [as the successor to the Prophet]." Thus a number of prominent Companions, including some of 'Alī's well-known supporters, refused to give allegiance to Abū Bakr. Ya'qūbī further reports that when Abū Bakr and 'Umar learned of the gathering of 'Alī's supporters in Fāṭimah's house, they went with other men intending to break into the house by force if necessary. 'Alī came out with his sword unsheathed. 'Umar, however, forced the sword out of his hand and broke it. Fāṭimah then came out and threatened 'Umar and his men saying, "By God, either you leave, or I will uncover my hair and cry out to God."[26]

In his account, Ṭabarī links 'Alī's refusal of allegiance to Abū Bakr to Fāṭimah's disagreement with the latter over her inheritance of the date palm orchard of Fadak, which the Prophet had kept for himself and his family from the spoils of the Jewish oasis of Khaybar.[27] He relates on the authority of 'Ā'ishah, the Prophet's wife, that 'Alī and al-'Abbās went to Abū Bakr to demand the garden of Fadak as their inheritance from the Prophet. He told them:

> I did hear the Messenger of God say, "We prophets do not give any inheritance. Anything we leave behind must remain as public charity [*ṣadaqah*]." Still, the people of Muḥammad's house will have their share of this wealth. By God, I will never see anything that the Messenger of God did, but that I will do the same.[28]

Fāṭimah left Abū Bakr in a mood of resentment and did not speak to him the rest of her life. Soon after her death however, 'Alī gathered all the men of Hāshim at his house and sent for Abū Bakr. He addressed the Caliph saying:

> What prevented us from giving allegiance to you was not our denial of your virtue, nor was it envy of anything with which God has favored you. Rather we believe that we have a rightful share in this affair, which you have denied us.

26. al-Ya'qūbī, vol. 2, pp. 124–126.
27. For a discussion of this conflict see *E.I.*^{2}, s.v. "Fadak."
28. al-Ṭabarī, vol. 3, p. 208.

Abū Bakr wept and assured ʿAlī that he intended him and all the sons of Hāshim nothing but good.[29]

Ṭabarī, seeking to minimize the significance of ʿAlī's opposition, consciously stresses the complete consensus of all the Muslims regarding Abū Bakr's caliphate. He reports on the authority of Sayf b. ʿUmar that a man asked Saʿīd b. Zayd, one of the Prophet's Companions, "Did you witness the death of the Messenger of God?" "Yes," he answered. The man inquired further, "When did Abū Bakr receive the *bayʿah* [of the people]?" Saʿīd replied, "It was on the day the Messenger of God died. This was because the people did not wish to remain even for part of a day without unity [*jamāʿah*]." The man continued, "Did anyone oppose Abū Bakr?" "No," Saʿīd answered, "except one who would have been determined to secede from Islam, or was at the point of so doing. But God delivered them [the Muhājirūn] from the plot of the Anṣār." The man again asked, "Did any man of the Muhājirūn withhold his *bayʿah*?" "No, they all willingly followed one another to give allegiance to Abū Bakr without even being called to come," asserted Saʿīd.[30] This last account precludes any dissent after the Saqīfah event.

Indeed, the Saqīfah Debate and its aftermath are shrouded in confusion. For instance Ṭabarī, who is generally a middle-of-the-road historian, presents several contradictory accounts of ʿAlī's attitude; some of which, as we have mentioned, relate that ʿAlī gave the *bayʿah* reluctantly and only much later, while according to others he hastened to do so immediately after the Prophet's death. The confusion in the accounts is, perhaps, symptomatic of the situation that existed at the time of the Prophet's death.

It was argued earlier in this discussion that the Prophet died without leaving a clear political system. The institution of the caliphate was the product of the tribal genius of Arab society in which a chief enjoyed social prestige rather than political authority. It was

29. Ibid.
30. Ibid., p. 207.

therefore natural that social and tribal considerations often took precedence over religious ones. Only in ʿAlī's case do we see a somewhat clear interplay between the two. Moreover, it remains an open question as to whether Abū Bakr and ʿUmar actually wished to seize power or, maybe more likely, merely wished to forestall sedition and discord within the still fragile social structure of the Muslim community. Indeed, Masʿūdī reports a brief but instructive exchange between ʿAlī and Abū Bakr. ʿAlī protested, "You have defrauded us of our right and did not heed it!" Abū Bakr answered, "No, rather I feared sedition."[31]

Abū Bakr's fear was not unfounded. The threat of sedition was a real problem facing Muslim society following the death of the Prophet, and can be clearly seen in the ancient and narrow tribal interests and rivalries that competed fiercely with the principle of the brotherhood of faith on which Muḥammad had sought to build the new Islamic order. These tribal tensions continued unabated during the rule of the four "Rightly Guided" caliphs and contributed directly to the turbulence that characterized that normative period. They intensified further during Umayyad rule and were the most significant factor in the dynasty's downfall.

We have dwelt on the Saqīfah event and its aftermath at some length because, as has already been noted, it mirrors much of the period of the high caliphate, and harkens back to pre-Islamic feuds and conflicts among Arab tribes. Thus, what decided matters in favor of Abū Bakr was, in the end, the old rivalry between the Aws and Khazraj tribes. The deep mistrust between these two tribes, noted earlier, can be clearly discerned in a comment attributed to a man of the Aws who advised his fellow tribesmen to pledge allegiance to Abū Bakr, saying:

> By God, if the men of the Khazraj were to gain power over you once, they would forever claim superiority over you, and would never agree to share it with you![32]

31. ʿAlī b. al-Ḥusayn al-Masʿūdī, *Murūj al-dhahab wa-maʿādin al-jawhar*, ed. Charles Pellat, 7 vols. (Beirut: Publications de l'Université Libanaise, 1966–79), vol. 3, p. 42.
32. al-Ṭabarī, vol. 3, pp. 221–222.

These rivalries existed not only between tribes, but also within large tribes such as the Quraysh which consisted of a number of integral clans and houses competing for social and political supremacy. Such was the case in the protracted strife between the houses of Umayyah and Hāshim,[33] who were direct descendants of one ancestor, ʿAbd Manāf. Yet when a common cause presented itself, the deep hostility and conflict between the two houses was temporarily put aside.

Abū Sufyān, a notable of the Umayyad house, had led the fight against Islam and its Prophet largely because Muḥammad was of the house of Hāshim. He grudgingly accepted the new faith when he had no other choice. When he learnt of the election of Abū Bakr, a Taymite, he could hardly contain his anger. "By God," he declared, "I see an upheaval that only blood will calm!" He then recalled the rivalry between the sons of ʿAbd Manāf and the rest of the Quraysh: "O sons of ʿAbd Manāf, how could you accept Abū Bakr to sit in authority over you?" Abū Sufyān taunted his fellow clansmen saying, "Where are the two weaklings! Where are the two most humiliated of men, ʿAlī and al-ʿAbbās!" He then turned to ʿAlī and said, "Put out your hand that I may give you *bayʿah*." But ʿAlī rebuked him saying, "By God, you seek nothing by this except sedition." Abū Sufyān asked, "Why has this affair gone to the least of the houses of the Quraysh? By God, if you so wish I will fill Madīnah with men and horses against him!" But ʿAlī again reproached Abū Sufyān saying, "Though you have always had nothing but animosity towards Islam and its people, yet you can cause it no harm. We consider Abū Bakr worthy of the caliphate."[34]

Ṭabarī's account of ʿAlī's mild opposition to Abū Bakr's leadership and his equally mild reluctance resistance in accepting it is, no doubt, apologetic. ʿAlī in fact appears to have never doubted his own right to the caliphate or his ability to shoulder its responsibilities. Nor could the religious grounds for the legitimacy of his claim be ignored. In any case, the important issue for our purpose is that by pledging allegiance

33. For a discussion of the history of this rivalry, see Maqrīzī, pp. 8 ff.
34. al-Ṭabarī, vol. 3, p. 209.

to Abū Bakr, he put the interests of the community and its unity above his own ideas and interests.

Furthermore, 'Alī and his opponents shared a common religious and moral commitment, which in the end would have made any one of them acceptable to the people. With a growth in power and wealth, however, the commitment of many of the Prophet's Companions to safeguard the integrity of the community began to wane. The crisis deepened and tragedy set in. As we shall presently see, Abū Bakr, 'Umar, 'Alī and other of the Companions were aware of this danger and did all they could to avert it. Yet it was the manner in which this first crisis was defused which set the stage for future trouble. The fear of the Anṣār of what was to come after Abū Bakr and 'Umar was more than justified.

3

Abū Bakr's Regrets and 'Umar's Uncertainties

Abū Bakr and 'Umar are known as the "two elders" (*shaykhayn*) of the Muslim community. Despite the tensions and intimidations that attended the Saqīfah Debate, it can still be argued that Abū Bakr and 'Umar ruled by moral suasion and mutual consultation rather than political power or naked coercive force. They did not seek wealth and pleasure or domination over their fellow Muslims, but endeavored to preserve the integrity of the new community and its unity, and to carry its message to the world. They were first among equals, disciplined by the time-honored Arab tribal tradition of equality among the free men of the tribe and the principles of gentleness and consultation that the Qur'ān had enjoined upon the Prophet of Islam and his community.[1]

Precepts of equality and mutual consultation, however, could operate effectively only in a cohesive society governed not by political interests and expediencies, but by moral imperatives and religious principles. That such principles and imperatives were foremost in the minds of a number of the Prophet's Companions is explicit in their insistence on equality and justice, moral and religious uprightness, and above all in their openness to criticism and their self-examining

1. See, for example, Q.3:159 and 42:38.

approach to power and its consequences. This attitude, which stemmed from fear of transgression and accountability before God on the Day of Judgment, resulted in feelings of regret and uncertainty in the minds of the two shaykhs regarding crucial decisions they made – decisions that were to shape subsequent Islamic history.

Abū Bakr: Khalīfat Rasūl Allāh

Ya'qūbī reports that Abū Bakr sat on the *minbar* – the Prophet's pulpit or seat of authority – a step lower than where the Prophet used to sit.[2] This act was no doubt meant to signify his humility, which is also reflected in his inaugural speech as the "first successor (*khalīfah*) of the Messenger of God." He said, as related on the authority of the famous Companion and traditionist Anas b. Mālik:

> O people, I have been given authority over you; yet, I am not the best of you. If I do good, assist me, but if I err, then you must set me straight. Obey me so long as I obey God and His Messenger. But if I disobey God and His Messenger, then you are under no obligation of obedience to me. I am only one like you. I do not know, perhaps you may charge me with things that only the Messenger of God could endure. God chose Muḥammad over humankind and protected him from all faults. As for me, I am a follower, and not an innovator."[3]

Abū Bakr's short caliphate was a transitional rule largely taken up with the wars of secession (*riddah*) within the greater Muslim community. At the same time, tensions between the Immigrants of the Quraysh and the Supporters of Madīnah continued to rise. The Anṣār for a while expressed their dissatisfaction by deserting Abū Bakr. Still, he did not wish to antagonize them, or deny them their high status. But when he praised them in his first address from the Prophet's pulpit, the men of the Quraysh were angry and asked 'Amr b. al-'Āṣ, who was a good orator, to deliver a speech disparaging the Anṣār. Abū Bakr later consulted 'Amr as to who should be entrusted with the standard of the

2. al-Ya'qūbī, vol. 2, p. 127.
3. al-Ṭabarī, vol. 3, pp. 210, 223. This and another of Abū Bakr's sermons is quoted more extensively in Appendix I.

army against the secessionist tribes. ʿAmr suggested the famous general Khālid b. al-Walīd of the Quraysh. Thābit b. Shammās, a notable of the Anṣār and one of their spokesman, protested:

> O men of the Quraysh, is there no one among us who is capable of what you are capable? By God, we are not blind to what we see, nor deaf to what we hear. But the Messenger of God commanded us to be patient, and we shall be patient.[4]

The Muslim state in its early stages was governed not by a complex and sophisticated political apparatus, as has already been observed, but by old tribal custom (*ʿurf*) and tradition (*taqlīd* or *sunnah*). In such an open system, political, social, and economic decisions were made collectively by the men of the tribe or tribal federation, not individually by the ruler and his small council or cabinet. The politicization of state affairs in the nascent Muslim community began in earnest not in Madīnah, but in Damascus under Muʿāwiyah and his Umayyad descendants. The two greatest problems that Abū Bakr and his successors had to face were the delimitation of the powers of the ruler and the management of the treasury (*bayt al-māl*), including the distribution of its contents. The displeasure of the Anṣār at being left out of political and military decisions has already been noted. However, Abū Bakr was able to avoid economic problems by observing strict equality in the distribution of wealth and booty.

Abū Bakr, we are told, divided the contents of the treasury equally among all the people. He allowed himself and his family the small sum of three dirhams a day only because he could no longer make his living through trade or farming. We are also told that before his death Abū Bakr directed that a date palm orchard he owned be sold to pay his debt to the public treasury. Describing his attitude towards wealth and worldly possessions, he declared:

> I have acquired nothing of your world. I have acted with regard to God's wealth and the affairs of the Muslims as would a guardian over the wealth of an orphan: if he enjoys riches he restrains himself, and if he suffers

4. al-Yaʿqūbī, vol. 2, p. 129.

want he observes decency and moderation [*ma'rūf*] in what he consumes of it.[5]

Both in the Saqīfah Debate, as we saw, and throughout Abū Bakr's brief caliphate, 'Umar played a decisive role. In fact the two men worked closely together, and Abū Bakr's gentle and emotional temperament was often balanced by 'Umar's strong personality and unshakeable determination. Thus when Abū Bakr wished, in compliance with the Prophet's orders from his death bed, to dispatch an army under the leadership of Usāmā b. Zayd to Syria against the Byzantines, he requested the young leader to leave 'Umar behind to assist him in his administrative duties. It was natural, therefore, that when Abū Bakr fell ill and the question of succession again came to the fore he appointed 'Umar as his successor. Abū Bakr asked 'Abd al-Raḥmān b. 'Awf what he thought of 'Umar as a possible candidate, and the latter answered, "He is better than you think, but he is somewhat harsh." Abū Bakr replied, "This is because he sees me as a soft man. Were he to take charge of this affair, he would surely temper his demeanor."[6]

Having assured Abū Bakr that 'Umar was a pious and good man, 'Abd al-Raḥmān consoled him saying, "Have no regrets regarding this ephemeral world." Abū Bakr replied:

> I have no regrets except for three things that I did, and wish I had not done; three things that I did not do, but wish I had done; and three things concerning which I wish I had enquired of the Messenger of God.

Two of the things that Abū Bakr regretted doing concern us here. He said:

> I wish that I had not been burdened with this office, but instead had brought 'Umar to the fore. It would have been better for me to be a subordinate [*wazīr*] rather than a commander [*amīr*]. I also wish that I had not searched the house of Fāṭimah, daughter of the Messenger of God, or allowed men to enter it, even if it was shut for the purpose of inciting war.

5. Ibid., pp. 136–137.
6. al-Ṭabarī, vol. 3, p. 428.

The three things that Abū Bakr wished he had done relate to administrative matters. As for the things that he wished he had asked the Prophet to clarify, he said:

> I wish that I had asked the Messenger of God who should take charge of this affair after him, so that no one could contest his claim to it. I also wish that I had asked, "Do the Anṣār have any share in it?"[7]

The fact that Ya'qūbī, an early Shī'ī historian reports this exchange is especially significant. First, it depicts an ambivalent, but generally sympathetic Shī'ī attitude towards Abū Bakr. This attitude gradually hardened, so that the two elders of the Quraysh, Abū Bakr and 'Umar, became the focus of Shī'ī–Sunni polemics.

Second, this colloquy, when considered with 'Umar's reservations concerning Abū Bakr's *bay'ah*, shows the uncertainty and confusion that surrounded the transition from prophetic to caliphal rule. Under the Prophet's tutelage, Madīnah was a veritable theocracy. Under the caliphs, the Muslim state was transformed first into a tribal meritocracy, then into a cosmopolitan nomocratic kingship, and finally into many and often disparate modern nation states.

Third, this report may have been intended to legitimize 'Umar's caliphate as part of the process of legitimizing the normative caliphate of the four "Rightly Guided" caliphs. The early development of this process is graphically depicted by the famous genealogist al-Zubayri who relates that Abū Bakr lost consciousness as he was dictating his last testament to 'Uthmān b. 'Affān. On regaining consciousness, Abū Bakr asked, "What would you have done had I died before this [final instruction]?" 'Uthmān answered, "Here is 'Umar's name, for I have already written it." Abū Bakr said, "You did the right thing, may God have mercy upon you. Had you written your own name, you would have been worthy of it [i.e., the caliphate]."[8]

Abū Bakr's caliphate was a formative period of consolidation and

7. al-Ya'qūbī, vol. 2, p. 137.
8. Abū 'Abd Allāh Muṣ'ab b. 'Abd Allāh b. Muṣ'ab al-Zubayrī, *Nasab Quraysh*, ed. A. Levi Provincal, 3rd edn. (Cairo: Dār al-Ma'ārif, n.d.), vol. 3, p. 104.

integration. The Riddah Wars not only ensured continuity with the Prophet's rule, they also inadvertently linked that continuity to an economic incentive through the promise of booty. In addition, they provided the necessary discipline and training for the highly motivated army which was to achieve vast conquests for the new Muslim state. Abū Bakr is reported to have perceived the dangers inherent in these developments: wealth and power and the possibility of vast conquests could threaten the moral and religious basis of Muslim society. He rebuked the men of the Quraysh for seeking to reduce the moral authority of the caliphate to one of political and economic power and tribal prestige. He was convinced that 'Umar was the best man to stem these dangers and keep the community on a straight course:

> I have chosen for the management of your affairs one who is the best of you in my estimation. Yet you all feel slighted because each of you wanted this office for himself. You anticipate great worldly wealth and prosperity, although prosperity has not yet come. Indeed it shall come, so that you will sleep on cushions of silk brocade behind silk curtains. By God, it is better for a man to have his head cut off, without it being a punishment [*ḥadd*] for a transgression, than to be swept up in the pleasures of this world! You shall be the first among the people to go astray and to hinder others from the straight way.[9]

This prophetic prediction, put in the mouth of the first caliph of Islam, describes well the lifestyle of a Muslim aristocracy made richer by lucrative posts in an ever expanding state. It also expresses the feelings of many pious Muslims about all political authority, including the caliphal office.

'Umar: Amīr al-Mu'minīn

'Umar was the first actual ruler or head of the Muslim state. He was the first to be called "*amīr al-mu'minīn*" ("Commander of the Faithful") instead of the more cumbersome, and increasingly less meaningful, designation "Successor of the Successor of the Messenger of God." Also symbolic of the transition from prophetic rule to Muslim

9. al-Ṭabarī, vol. 3, pp. 429–430.

state was his first significant administrative act, which was to fix the Islamic calendar for the purpose of dating state records and important events and documents.[10] His ten-year rule was a period of great expansion and prosperity with all the temptations and demographic problems these entailed. ʿUmar perceived the problems and temptations and sought to deal with them. He was certainly a political genius, but he lacked Abū Bakr's vision and gentleness.

As state revenues increased due to conquests, ʿUmar turned his attention to the thorny problem of allotment (*ʿaṭāʾ*) of this vast wealth. The suggestions of two of the Companions whom he consulted on this matter are instructive in that they indicate the two social and administrative choices open to the community. ʿAlī proposed that whatever wealth was accumulated should be equally divided amongst all the Muslims, without anything being kept in the treasury. In this he followed the practice of the Prophet and Abū Bakr. ʿUthmān counselled that records be kept of what each individual was to receive and that the treasury not be left empty, there being enough wealth for everyone. ʿUmar accepted the latter advice, established financial state registers (*dīwāns*) and recruited an army of paid professional soldiers. In this he followed the pattern of state administration that he observed in Syria.[11] He thus began the process of actual state-building in Islam.

ʿUmar did not, as did his two predecessors the Prophet and Abū Bakr, distribute the wealth of the Muslims equally among them. This change in policy was to have far-reaching consequences as it set a precedent for later and much more flagrant violations of the important principle of equality. In the year 20/640–41, following two years of drought and famine, ʿUmar is reported to have adhered to a graded principle of preference in the allotment of wealth. He preferred those who had priority in accepting Islam over other Muslims; the Muhājirūn of the Quraysh over other Immigrants; all the Muhājirūn

10. See ibid., vol. 4, p. 39; al-Yaʿqūbī, vol. 2, p. 145.
11. al-Ṭabarī, vol. 4, pp. 209–210.

over all the Anṣār; and the Aws of the Anṣār over the Khazraj. He also preferred the Muḍar of the Arabs over those of Rabīah and Yaman, Arabs over non-Arabs, and freemen over their slaves or clients (*mawālī*). Among the Prophet's wives, 'Umar likewise preferred the daughters of the men of Quraysh over others. 'Umar's general principle was to begin with the nearest blood or marriage relatives of the Prophet in the allotment of wealth. He insisted, however, on placing himself and his family "where God had placed them," farthest removed from the Prophet genealogically, and without regard to his own status as the Commander of the Faithful.

In the end 'Umar realized the inequity that this practice of social stratification entailed. He thus declared:

> I had sought to placate people by preferring some of them over others. But if I live this year, I will observe equality among all people and will not prefer any person over another. I will follow the example of the Messenger of God and Abū Bakr.[12]

'Umar died before he could implement this important measure of social and economic reform. Thus his principle of preference, which implied the superiority of some men of the Quraysh over others, of the Quraysh over all Arabs, and of Arabs over non-Arabs, took precedence over the Qur'ānic principle of the equality of all the people of faith, a principle that the Prophet had used to distinguish between the *jāhiliyyah*, or time of folly and wrongdoing, and *islām*. 'Umar is said to have realized that inequality constituted a reversion to the time of *jāhiliyyah* and to have castigated the people with these strong words:

> It has come to me that you hold assemblies, but that no two men come together without each one boasting, "I am of the companions of so and so," or "I am a member of the assembly of so and so." People have thus

12. al-Ya'qūbī, vol. 2, pp. 152–154; al-Ṭabarī, vol. 4, pp. 209 ff. Ṭabarī records all this under the year 23, but does not report 'Umar's decision to abandon this practice. See also the interesting discussion of this in Muḥammad Mahdī Shams al-Dīn, *Thawrat al-Ḥusayn: ẓurūfuhā al-ijtimā' iyyah wa-āthuruhā al-insāniyyah*, 5th edn. (Beirut: Dār al-Ta'āruf, 1398/1978), pp. 28–30.

> come to shun assemblies. By God, this will quickly destroy your religion, your honor and your unity![13]

It was in fact this kind of social stratification that reduced the sacred office of the *khilāfah*, or vicegerency of God and His Messenger, to a monarchy – and Muslim society to a society of oppressive masters and oppressed slaves.

As the Muslim state grew, social prestige and economic prosperity increasingly depended on government posts and military services. Soon after the death of 'Umar, the men of the Quraysh, being by nature adventurous traders, made of such posts and services a lucrative business. This too undermined the people's faith-commitment and moral conscience. Again, 'Umar wisely anticipated this danger and forbade the men of the Quraysh to leave Madīnah on *jihād*, or military expeditions. He argued that the men of the Quraysh had done enough *jihād* with the Messenger of God and then declared, "I shall take the men of the Quraysh by the throat at the entrances of this city, so that they will not be able to leave!"[14]

The issue of succession was more of a problem for 'Umar than it had been for Abū Bakr. This was partly because there was no generally accepted Prophetic precedence or clear Qur'ānic dictum for the community to follow in choosing a successor, partly because of the rapid and extensive expansion of the community, and partly because the Arab tribes which made up the community were not yet sufficiently politicized to accept the dictates of a higher political office. The fragility of the concept of a supratribal politics may be observed in the hostility that the people of Kūfah showed towards 'Ammār b. Yāsir who was a prominent Companion, but a black man and not of the Quraysh. 'Umar appointed him as governor of Kūfah, but had to recall him because the people would not tolerate a black man ruling over them.[15] With no established process for the transfer of caliphal power, 'Umar

13. al-Ṭabarī, vol. 4, p. 213.
14. al-Ya'qūbī, vol. 2, pp. 157–158.
15. al-Ṭabarī, vol. 4, pp. 165–166.

was caught between his own policy of creating tribal stratification within the community and the need to re-establish the principle of a singular unified Muslim *ummah*. He appears to have thought it inadvisable to apply the principle of open consultation in choosing his successor, as this could have resulted in chaos and open conflict. Nor did he turn to a simple form of tribal/family appointment.

In his allotment of wealth 'Umar had given first priority to the Banū Hāshim because of their close kinship to the Prophet. He may have wished to apply the same principle with regard to high administrative positions, but he hesitated because he recalled that the Prophet had not appointed any of his close relatives to such posts. 'Umar wished to appoint 'Abd Allāh Ibn 'Abbās, whom he held in high regard on account of his learning, as his governor over the district of Ḥimṣ. In the end, he dismissed the idea because, he said, "I see that the Messenger of God appointed other men and left you." Ibn 'Abbās agreed. 'Umar continued:

> By God, I do not know what to think! Did he consider you [the men of Banū Hāshim] unfit for such posts, although you are indeed capable, or did he fear that men would give *bay'ah* to you on account of your close kinship to him? Then much gossip would have ensued.[16]

'Umar may not have wished the men of Banū Hāshim to become the focus of conflict over the question of succession; but, it is more likely that he did not want 'Alī, or for that matter any Hashimite, to be elevated to the office of the caliphate.

The problem of succession increasingly became a source of trouble and uncertainty for 'Umar. Again this may be, as the early historian of Madīnah 'Umar b. Shabbah (d. 262/876) reports, because 'Umar found no clear precedent to follow. His son 'Abd Allāh communicated to him the people's dissatisfaction with his indecision, whereupon he replied, "If I do not appoint a successor, neither did the Messenger of God; and if I do, then I see that Abū Bakr did appoint his successor." 'Abd Allāh is said to have concluded, "When he mentioned the Prophet, I knew

16. al-Mas'ūdī, vol. 3, pp. 65–66.

that he would not override the action of the Messenger of God."[17] Thus, while 'Umar had shown himself to be a capable and decisive ruler, on his deathbed he acted indecisively in dealing with this difficult problem.

Perhaps recognizing the explosive nature of the issue of succession, 'Umar left the question in abeyance and entrusted the matter to a consultative (*shūrā*) committee comprised of all likely candidates. In a highly interesting private colloquy between 'Umar and Ibn 'Abbās, the former gave the following assessment of the main candidates for the caliphate after his death.

Ibn 'Abbās first suggested 'Abd al-Raḥmān b. 'Awf, but 'Umar objected, "He is a stingy man, and this office needs one who gives without being extravagant, and withholds without being too frugal." Of Sa'd b. Abī Waqqāṣ, 'Umar said that he was a good but weak man. He objected to Ṭalḥah b. 'Abd Allāh because, he said, "He loves praise so much that he would spend his own wealth and even that of others on obtaining it." 'Umar rejected al-Zubayr, even though he was a great warrior, because, "He is one day a human being and one day a devil," and also because he was too scheming.

Although it casts doubt over the entire colloquy, as it strongly suggests that the whole dialogue was written long after the fact, 'Umar's assessment of 'Uthmān is interesting. He is reported to have said:

> Were the son of Abū Mu'ayṭ [that is 'Uthmān] to be entrusted with the caliphate, he would favor the men of Banū Umayyah at the expense of the rest of the people. If he does this the Arabs will attack him in his house and kill him.[18]

'Umar's assessment of 'Alī's character and leadership potential is is no less interesting, and likewise subject to doubt. 'Umar, according to this account, waited for Ibn 'Abbās to speak on 'Alī's behalf. As the

17. Abū Zayd 'Umar b. Shabbah al-Namīrī al-Baṣrī, *Ta'rīkh al-madīna al-munawwarah akhbār al-madīnah al-nabawiyyah*, ed. Muḥammad Shaltūt, 4 vols. (Makkah: Dār al-Turāth, 1399/1979), vol. 2, p. 885.
18. al-Ya'qūbī, vol. 2, p. 158; see also Ibn Shabbah, vol. 2, pp. 880–881.

latter hesitated, 'Umar prompted him saying, "Out with it, Ibn 'Abbās! Do you think your fellow is suitable?" Ibn 'Abbās replied, "How could he be not suitable considering his excellence and priority [in Islam], his close kinship [with the Prophet] and his learning?" 'Umar agreed:

> He is, by God, as you say. Were he to hold this office, he would lead the people on the right way and follow a clear course. Yet he possesses some [negative] qualities. He is given to jest in assembly, headstrong, reproachful towards others, and too young.

Ibn 'Abbās retorted:

> O Commander of the Faithful, did you think him too young on the day of the Trench [6/627], when 'Amr b. 'Abd Widd came forth challenging your great warriors and all the swordsmen held back and no one dared face him [except 'Alī]? And what about the day of Badr when 'Alī struck off heads in great numbers?

'Umar became angry, and Ibn 'Abbās held his peace. Finally 'Umar conceded that 'Alī was most worthy of the caliphate, remarking however that, "The people of the Quraysh would not tolerate him." This was because, 'Umar argued, "Were he to rule over them, he would deal with them in accordance with the bitter truth; nor would they find any leniency in him. They would surely then revoke their allegiance to him, and fighting would ensue."[19] According to Ibn Shabbah's version of this report, 'Alī was given to vanity and jest. Still, 'Umar asserted that 'Alī would be more certain than all the other men to rule the Muslims in accordance "with the Book of God and *sunnah* of their Prophet."[20]

We have quoted this colloquy at some length for several reasons. First, it reflects not so much what 'Umar may or may not have said, but his attitude as well as that of later Muslims towards the changing office of the caliphate. 'Umar in the end did not, as we shall see, wish to be directly involved in what he perceived as a difficult situation. Secondly, historians, traditionists, jurists, and indeed the generality of

19. Ibid., p. 159.
20. Ibn Shabbah, vol. 2, pp. 882–883.

Muslims, felt it necessary to defend the right of both ʿAlī and ʿUthmān to the caliphate. Finally, although the account itself may be apocryphal, it nonetheless presents the main points of long and bitter polemics between the Shīʿah (the "party" of ʿAlī) and the Umayyads and their supporters, and in the end between Shīʿī and Sunni Islam.

4

The Second Crisis: The Shūrā Council and its Failure

The first crisis of Muslim history following the death of the Prophet Muḥammad was largely an institutional crisis. But, as has already been observed, the caliphate provided a highly original and natural solution to this problem. The second crisis was then, and has remained to the present, a crisis of legitimate authority. The first crisis centered around the problem of transition from a theocratic rule based on revelation (the Qur'ān) and on the Prophet's *sunnah* (dictates and conduct), which was itself guided by the Qur'ān. The second, and far more serious crisis, was a struggle between men of wealth and prestige and less privileged men who insisted on approximating the prophetic model of government at all cost, without any regard for changing socio-political and economic conditions. We saw how both Abū Bakr and 'Umar realized the great danger of the temptations of power and wealth, and warned the people of the possibility of sedition (*fitnah*) which could destroy the social and moral fabric of the community. Unfortunately history bore the "two shaykhs" out, and the period following 'Umar's caliphate has been aptly characterized by the late Egyptian thinker Ṭāhā Ḥusayn as the age of "the great *fitnah*."[1]

1. Ṭāhā Ḥusayn's two-volume work *al-Fitnah al-kubrā* (Cairo: Dār al-Ma'ārif, 1966) examines the period of 'Uthmān's and 'Alī's caliphates, and their aftermath.

We saw in the Saqīfah Debate that the main argument against the Anṣār in favor of Abū Bakr's caliphate rested on the priority of the Quraysh over all other Muslims. Yet neither Abū Bakr nor 'Umar adopted this as a binding principle. Rather, the primary consideration remained near kinship to the Prophet coupled with piety, moral uprightness, and religious knowledge. It was such considerations and the fear of dissension that, in our view, led 'Umar not to choose a successor himself, but rather to leave the matter of choice to six men well-known for their piety and social prestige. 'Umar's decision, moreover, to limit deliberations on this weighty matter to only six men, instead of making it an open consultation (*shūrā*) or simply himself appointing his successor, as did Abū Bakr, was in all probability due to his uncertainty as to who would be the most suitable man after him for an office of ever-increasing power and influence. The *shūrā* committee was in some respects, as we shall presently see, an unfortunate way out of this dilemma.

When it became certain that 'Umar would die of the wound inflicted upon him by a disgruntled and ambitious Persian slave, he was advised, we are told, to appoint a successor. It was suggested that he appoint his son 'Abd Allāh, a man highly respected for his piety and integrity, but 'Umar angrily rejected this proposal. He is said to have agonized over the question of succession saying:

> Who should I appoint as successor? Were Abū 'Ubaydah b. al-Jarrāḥ still alive, I would appoint him; and if my Lord then questioned me about him, I would reply, "I heard your Prophet say that Abū 'Ubaydah was the trustful man [*amīn*] of this community."

'Umar is also reported to have considered worthy for the caliphal office a man called Sālim, a client or slave (*mawlā*) of the Companion Abū Ḥudhayfah, because he heard the Prophet say, "Sālim loves God exceedingly." 'Umar would have likewise considered Mu'ādh b. Jabal and Khālid b. al-Walīd, had they still been alive: Mu'ādh, because 'Umar heard the Prophet praise him for his great learning; Khālid, because the Prophet had once said of him "Khālid b. al-Walīd is one of God's swords that He has unsheathed against the Associators [*mushrikūn*] [of other things with God]."[2]

This account raises several important questions. First, why did 'Umar not think any of his fellow Companions good enough to appoint as successor? And why, at the same time, did he appoint six men as possible candidates, when he considered none of them fit for the caliphate? Second, if only the men of the Quraysh were fit for caliphal office, then why did 'Umar wish he could have appointed Sālim, who was only a *mawlā* of a man of the Quraysh, or Mu'ādh, who was of the tribe of Khazraj? Finally, why did 'Umar exclude his son, even though he would have been acceptable to many of the men of the Quraysh? Our discussion so far has already suggested partial answers to these questions. But because we are primarily interested in the attitudes and motivations behind the religio-political situation in early Islam, it will be necessary to stay with these questions a while longer.

'Umar was no doubt a farsighted man who could see that, in the absence of a generally accepted political direction, whatever he and Abū Bakr did would set a precedent for later generations. He therefore regretted Abū Bakr's manner of appointment, calling it "an evil slip." He is also said to have warned: "Kill anyone who attempts another like it!"[3]

Balādhurī describes well the widespread apprehension concerning the appointments of both Abū Bakr and 'Umar, and the latter's own awareness of this general mood of uncertainty. He reports 'Umar complaining: "There are men who say that Abū Bakr's *bay'ah* was a slip, but that God has averted its evil, and that 'Umar's *bay'ah* was concluded without consultation. Therefore, this matter shall be decided after me through consultation."[4] This may explain why 'Umar, after much hesitation, decided against appointing a successor himself. When it was suggested that he should choose someone to succeed him,

2. al-Ṭabarī, vol. 4, p. 227; Ibn Qutaybah, vol. 1, p. 28.
3. See Chapter 2, p. 15, note 19; also, al-Ya'qūbī, vol. 2, p. 158.
4. al-Balādhurī, *Ansāb al-ashrāf*, 6 vols. (Wiesbaden: Frantis Steiner [Publications of the German Oriental Institute, Beirut]), vol. 2, ed. Ihsan 'Abbās, 1979, p. 500.

appoint his own son, or at least leave a testament concerning this matter, he said:

> We have no desire to lord over you. I have never appreciated it [i.e. the caliphate] so that I would wish it for any other man of my house. If it is a good thing, we have had our share of it. But if it is evil, then it is better for 'Umar's family that only one man be brought to judgment and questioned concerning the affairs of Muḥammad's community. I have surely exerted myself and deprived my family. If, therefore, I may be spared [on the Day of Judgment], without either reward or punishment, it will be sufficient for me, and I will be happy. I will not bear this [burden] both during my life and after I die.[5]

Abū Bakr, 'Umar, 'Alī and others of the Prophet's companions regarded the caliphate not as an office for material gain and social status, but as a commitment to the service of God and His servants. Others, however, as will be amply demonstrated below, regarded the caliphate as kingship (*mulk*), God's wealth as their wealth and God's servants as their subservient subjects. Thus the office of the representative (*khalīfah*) of the Messenger of God was transformed into an autocratic power.

The two problems that 'Umar appears to have feared most were nepotism and hereditary rule. He sought to forestall the second problem by refusing to appoint his son as his successor, or to include any of his relatives in the *shūra* council.[6] With regard to the problem of nepotism, he insisted that whoever was chosen for the caliphate must not favor his own relatives at the expense of the people. 'Umar's efforts were, however, to no avail. Soon nepotism was to create the first "great *fitnah*" in the Muslim *ummah*, and hereditary rule was to turn the caliphate into a dynastic monarchy and thus a source of much intrigue and tragedy.

5. al-Ṭabarī, vol. 4, p. 227.
6. This was his reason for excluding Sa'īd ibn Zayd ibn 'Umar ibn Nufayl. See ibid., vol. 4, pp. 227–228; al-Ya'qūbī, vol. 2, p. 159.

The Shūrā Deliberations

The six men 'Umar appointed as members of the *shūrā* council were 'Alī and 'Uthmān, the two descendants of 'Abd Manāf – the progenitor of both Umayyah and Hāshim – and sons-in-law of the Prophet; 'Abd al-Raḥmān b. 'Awf and Sa'd b. Abī Waqqāṣ, the Prophet's maternal uncles; al-Zubayr b. al-'Awwām, the Prophet's cousin; and Ṭalḥah b. 'Abd Allāh, whom the Prophet had called "Ṭalḥah the good." It appears that 'Umar believed 'Alī and 'Uthmān to be the strongest caliphal candidates. Some historians even suggest that he was personally more inclined towards 'Alī. He is reported to have said before his death, "I have decided to consider the matter and appoint a man to manage your affairs who would be most worthy among you to deal justly with you," and then to have pointed to 'Alī.[7]

It seems more likely, however, that 'Umar refused to set a precedent whereby every caliph after him would appoint his own successor. He is reported to have remarked to his son 'Abd Allāh, "If they choose for it [the caliphate] this bald man ['Alī], he would lead them on the right course." His son asked, "What prevents you from appointing him, O Commander of the Faithful?" 'Umar answered, "I will not bear this burden both alive and dead."[8]

It must be observed that 'Umar was married to Umm Kulthūm, 'Alī's daughter by Fāṭimah, which indicates an amicable relation between the two men. This fact has led a well-known modern Shī'ī thinker to conclude that 'Umar was inclined to appoint 'Alī as caliph after him, and that he was prevented from carrying out his plan by the success of an Umayyad plot to have him assassinated and 'Uthmān installed in his place.[9] This is no doubt a fanciful conjecture that cannot be substantiated, but which is, nonetheless, an intriguing one.

'Umar's choice of these six men appears to have been deliberate and consonant with his hierarchical view of society. The suggestion that he

7. al-Ṭabarī, vol. 4, p. 227.
8. al-Balādhurī, vol. 2, p. 501.
9. See Hāshim Ma'rūf al-Ḥasanī, *al-Intifāḍāt al-shī'iyyah 'abr al-tarīkh* (Beirut: Dār al-Kutub al-Sha'biyyah, n.d.), pp. 50–51.

inclined towards 'Alī notwithstanding, his selection of the men for the *shūrā* council weighted the outcome in favor of 'Uthmān. 'Umar, furthermore, may not have completely perceived the far-reaching religious, political, social, and economic consequences of his action, thinking the committee representing the various trends within the Qurayshi aristocracy could resolve the issue before his death. He thus called the five men (Ṭalḥah being absent at the time) and exhorted them saying:

> I have carefully pondered this matter and found you to be the chiefs of the people and their leaders. Nor should this affair be entrusted to anyone except you. I do not fear men with regard to you if you yourselves are upright. But I fear disagreement amongst you; then the people would fall into dissension.[10]

'Umar then instructed the men to meet nearby and quickly choose one man from among themselves. But, as he heard them loudly arguing without arriving at a decision, he set strict rules for them to follow in their deliberations after his death.[11] 'Umar, reports Balādhurī, also spoke privately to 'Alī and 'Uthmān. To 'Alī he said:

> It may be that these men will recognize your close kinship to the Prophet, your status as his son-in-law and the great knowledge and understanding with which God has favored you. If therefore you are appointed to this office, then fear God in managing it.

He then said to 'Uthmān:

> Perhaps these men will recognize your status as the Prophet's son-in-law and your venerable old age. Thus, if you are chosen for this office, then fear God and do not set the sons of Abū Mu'ayṭ [that is his Umayyad relatives] over the necks of the people.[12]

It was observed above that 'Umar, perhaps unknowingly, weighted the result of the council's deliberations in favor of 'Uthmān. Two important considerations have led us to this conclusion. The first is the actual makeup of the committee and the rules imposed on its members. The

10. al-Ṭabarī, vol. 4, p. 228.
11. Ibid., p. 229.
12. al-Balādhurī, vol. 2, p. 501.

second is 'Alī's acknowledged attitude towards the caliphate in general, and towards the claims of Abū Bakr and 'Umar in particular.

The council was constituted in such a way as to make its final conclusion almost inevitable. The logic of the situation is revealed in a highly significant exchange reported to have taken place between 'Alī and his venerable uncle, al-'Abbās. After 'Alī had agreed to be included in the *shūrā* council, al-'Abbās reproved him saying, "So you have turned away from us [that is his Hashimite kinsmen]!" Surprised by this reproach, 'Alī answered: "Umar placed 'Uthmān on a par with me and said to us, 'Be with the majority. But if two men choose one man and the other two men choose another, then side with the two who include 'Abd al-Raḥmān b. 'Awf.'"

He then commented:

> Sa'd would never oppose his cousin 'Abd al-Raḥmān. 'Abd al-Raḥmān, moreover, is 'Uthmān's brother-in-law. All three men, therefore, would never disagree among themselves. Thus either 'Abd al-Raḥmān will nominate 'Uthmān, or 'Uthmān will nominate 'Abd al-Raḥmān. In that case, even if the two other men [i.e. Ṭalḥah and al-Zubayr] were to side with me, they would avail me nothing and, in reality, I hold some hope in only one of them.

That 'Alī understood the dynamics and held no illusions as to the impartiality of the council is clear. That he understood and yet still accepted to join the deliberations is confusing and did nothing towards answering his uncle's accusation. Al-'Abbās's frustration and anger are patent in his response:

> I have not supported you in a cause, but that you came back to me faltering and with hateful results. I advised you, when the Messenger of God was on his deathbed, to ask him to whom this affair belongs, but you refused. Then after he died I advised you to make the decision quickly [that is to accept al-'Abbās's *bay'ah*], but you did not follow my advice. Again, when 'Umar named you among the men in the *shūrā* council, I advised you not to be included, but you refused.

And his assessment of the situation is contained in his final piece of advice to 'Alī: "Remember one thing, whatever these people present to you, say no, except if they choose you for the caliphate. Beware these men, for they will never cease opposing us in this matter until someone else is chosen for leadership over us." Al-'Abbās then warned his nephew of the evil consequences of such an outcome.[13]

Fully aware of the bias of the *shūrā* council, 'Alī chose to take his seat there and risk the displeasure of his supporters, for good reason. His absence from the council would have been more destructive of the community than his presence of his ascension to the caliphate. Implicit in this attitude is 'Alī's very different perspective. For him, the *shūrā* council was irrelevant; in his eyes the caliphate was not a question of politics, it was a question of moral prerogative. 'Alī was convinced of his sole right to the office; he did not accept the legitimacy of the claims of Abū Bakr and 'Umar; and, he regarded himself and his immediate family as the people of the household (*ahl al-bayt*) of the Prophet.[14] As head of the household, he was the Prophet's heir. He was further convinced that the men of the Quraysh were intent on subverting his right to his inheritance, the caliphate.

'Alī could not agree to base his own claim, albeit in part, on the model and precedent of his two predecessors. His widely acclaimed piety, wisdom, courage, austerity, and uncompromising egalitarianism set him apart from the rest of his fellow Muslims. He was a man of independent mind, unwilling to be bound by social precedent or custom. These characteristics, among others, provided his political opponents with good pretexts for excluding him; his almost apolitical stance made it easy for them. Together, these factors also provided the grounds and framework for the development of Shi'ism as an independent theological and political school within Islam.

When it became apparent that the *shūrā* council would not be able to resolve the issue before his death, 'Umar appointed his son, 'Abd Allāh, as an outside adviser and made 'Abd al-Raḥmān b. 'Awf the virtual head and final arbiter of the council. 'Abd al-Raḥmān quickly

13. al-Ṭabarī, vol. 4, pp. 229–230.
14. See Chapter 2, particularily the discussion of the Saqīfah Debate, and the surrounding text at p. 18.

excluded himself on condition that his decision would be binding on all the others. ʿUthmān agreed, but ʿAlī demanded: "Give me your word of honor that you will abide by the truth, that you will not follow your own caprice, that you will not favor a close relative, and that you will not spare any effort in your duty towards the community."[15] ʿAbd al-Raḥmān agreed, and began his consultations with the members of the council as well as the rest of the people. He talked privately to ʿAlī and asked him whom he would have chosen had he not been a candidate for the office. ʿAlī answered that he would have chosen ʿUthmān. ʿAbd al-Raḥmān put the same question to ʿUthmān, and the latter said that he would have favored ʿAlī. The majority of those consulted by ʿAbd al-Raḥmān were, according to most reports, inclined towards ʿUthmān.

On the morning of the third of the three days that ʿUmar had stipulated as the period for consultation, ʿAbd al-Raḥmān called Saʿd b. Abī Waqqāṣ and al-Zubayr and said to the latter, "Step aside and leave this matter to the two sons of ʿAbd Manāf." Al-Zubayr agreed and voted for ʿAlī. ʿAbd al-Raḥmān then said to Saʿd, "You and I are cousins, so leave your lot in this matter to me and let me choose." Saʿd replied, "Yes, but only if you choose yourself. But if you choose ʿUthmān, then I prefer ʿAlī." Saʿd then pleaded, "O man, choose yourself for this office and spare us more trouble and lift up our heads!" ʿAbd al-Raḥmān insisted that he had no desire for the office because he would be no match for Abū Bakr and ʿUmar.[16]

ʿAbd al-Raḥmān then called ʿUthmān and ʿAlī together with the notables of the Muhājirūn and Anṣār and urged them all to come to a decision and to avoid dissension. Saʿīd b. Zayd urged ʿAbd al-Raḥmān to assume the caliphate himself, but ʿAbd al-Raḥmān declined. Then ʿAmmār b. Yāsir, a staunch supporter of ʿAlī, suggested, "If you wish the Muslims not to fall into dissension, then give allegiance to ʿAlī!" Al-Miqdād b. al-Aswad, another strong supporter of ʿAlī, concurred:

15. al-Ṭabarī, vol. 4, p. 231.
16. Ibid.

"'Ammār is right. If you give allegiance to 'Alī, we would say 'We hear and we obey!'" 'Abd Allāh b. Abī Sarḥ, a notorious man of the Umayyads whose blood the Prophet had made lawful to shed,[17] declared, "If you wish the men of the Quraysh to not fall into dissension, then give allegiance to 'Uthmān!" Thus the argument quickly degenerated into a tribal squabble between Hashimites and Umayyads, and their respective supporters.[18]

As the choice was narrowed down to 'Alī and 'Uthmān, 'Abd al-Raḥmān stipulated that the candidate should meet three essential conditions. These were that he should abide by the Book of God and the *sunnah* of His Messenger, that he should follow the example of Abū Bakr and 'Umar, and that he should not favor his own relatives at the expense of the people. Historians present significantly different accounts of 'Alī's reaction to these conditions. Ya'qūbī reports that 'Abd al-Raḥmān met 'Alī and 'Uthmān privately and put the conditions to them. He said to 'Alī: "God is witness over you that if you assume this office you will deal with us in accordance with the Book of God, the *sunnah* of His Prophet and the example of Abū Bakr and 'Umar." 'Alī replied, "I will deal with you in accordance with the Book of God and the *sunnah* of His Prophet to the best of my ability." After 'Abd al-Raḥmān repeated the same demand the second and third time, 'Alī retorted, "With the Book of God and the *sunnah* of His Prophet there is no need for the example of anyone." Suspecting the motive behind 'Abd al-Raḥmān's insistence on a categorical answer to his demands, 'Alī said accusingly, "You are sparing no effort in subverting my right to this office!" 'Uthmān gave the

17. 'Abd Allāh b. Sa'd b. Abī Sarḥ was 'Uthmān's brother in nursing. He was employed for sometime by the Prophet as one of his scribes of revelation. But 'Abd Allāh used to alter what the Prophet dictated and to boast that he was writing the Qur'ān for Muḥammad. Thus on the day of the conquest of Makkah the Prophet ordered that he be executed. But 'Abd Allāh sought protection with 'Uthmān and was finally rehabilitated by him; al-Balādhurī, vol. 2, p. 539. See also Shihāb al-Dīn Aḥmad b. 'Alī b. Muḥammad Ibn Ḥajar al-'Asqalānī, *al-Iṣābah fī tamīyz al-ṣaḥābah*, 4 vols. (Beirut: Dār al-Fikr, 1398/1978), vol. 2, p. 316.
18. al-Ṭabarī, vol. 4, pp. 232–233.

required answer and received ʿAbd al-Raḥmān's *bayʿah*, and with it the caliphate.[19]

Ibn Qutaybah presents a much sharper exchange between ʿAlī and ʿAbd al-Raḥmān. The latter, we are told, made a pact with ʿUthmān that he would not burden the people with personal favors to his own relatives, and that he would follow the example of the two venerable shaykhs. ʿAlī, however, protested:

> What have you to do with the matter if you entrust me with this office? It will be my task to manage to the best of my ability the affairs of Muḥammad's community. Wherever I find strength and trustworthiness I will employ them, be they found in the men of Banū Hāshim or any other men.

ʿAbd al-Raḥmān insisted, "No, by God, not until you grant me this condition!" But ʿAlī was adamant; he persisted, "No, by God, I will never grant it to you."[20]

Ṭabarī's account of the encounter between ʿAlī and ʿAbd al-Raḥmān clearly indicates the latter's preference for ʿUthmān. Here, ʿUthmān is again made to give an unequivocal answer to ʿAbd al-Raḥmān's demands. But, in this telling, ʿAlī's more cautious reply does not amount to a rejection of ʿAbd al-Raḥmān's conditions. ʿAbd al-Raḥmān insisted: "You are bound by your pledge to God and by His covenant that you will follow the Book of God and the *sunnah* of His Messenger, as well as the example of his two successors." ʿAlī replied, "I hope to do so to the best of my knowledge and ability." But ʿAbd al-Raḥmān offered his *bayʿah* to ʿUthmān. Seeing this, ʿAlī angrily exclaimed, "This is not the first day that you make common cause against us!" Then citing the example of Joseph, son of Jacob, who was wronged by his brothers, he continued, "Fair patience and God's succor [we beseech] against what you claim" (Q.12:18). ʿAlī then concluded, "By God, you would not have chosen ʿUthmān for this office but that he would return you the favor later."[21]

19. al-Yaʿqūbī, vol. 2, p. 162.
20. Ibn Qutaybah, vol. 1, p. 45.
21. al-Ṭabarī, vol. 4, p. 233.

5

‘Uthmān: Khalīfat Allāh

‘Uthmān’s caliphate constituted a total break with tradition and ushered in a new era of Muslim history. It was a break with the pious and somewhat austere framework within which the two venerable elders, Abū Bakr and ‘Umar, served the people in that it transformed the caliphate from an essentially tribal-religious authority into an autocratic institution. It ushered in a new era in that it brought to power a new dynasty that would change the structure of Muslim society and alter the course of its history.

Abū Bakr, it should be remembered, saw himself as an inadequate but faithful representative (*khalīfah*) of the Messenger of God. Although ‘Umar chose the epithet “*amīr al-mu’minīn*” (“Commander of the Faithful”), he nonetheless saw himself as “the successor of the successor of the Messenger of God.” ‘Uthmān, in contrast, preferred the title *khalīfat Allāh* (God’s representative), and thus did not feel bound by the precedent of the two elders.[1] ‘Uthmān saw his rule as a God-given authority, resembling that of divine-right kingship rather than successorship (*khilīfah*) to the Prophet of God.

1. See Madelung, p. 80; also, Patricia Crone and Martin Hinds, *God’s Caliph* (London: Cambridge University Press, 1986), p. 21 *et passim*.

'Uthmān's Caliphate: Umayyad Power and the Beginning of Shī'ī Opposition

The twelve-year rule of 'Uthmān, the shaykh of the sons of Umayyah and twice son-in-law of the Prophet, was a period of intrigue and tragedy, of sedition and disenchantment. It led some among the Muslims to seek alternatives to the caliphal model and others to withdraw from social and political affairs altogether. Broadly speaking, the first group crystallized in Shi'ism, the second in Sufism. 'Uthmān's rule set the stage for a degree of schism and civil strife that shook the Muslim *ummah* to its foundations.

It was observed earlier that neither Abū Bakr nor 'Umar saw their rank on the Prophet's seat of authority (the *minbar*) as equal with their rank and status. Thus Abū Bakr sat a step lower than the Prophet, and 'Umar sat a step lower than Abū Bakr. 'Uthmān, we are told, sat on the topmost step, where the prophet used to sit. When people questioned him about this highly symbolic act, he simply replied that Abū Bakr and 'Umar had prepared the gesture for him. Some of the people present saw this as an ominous innovation, and one man observed, "Today evil was born." Ya'qūbī, who reported this event, added that as a result, some men were inclined towards 'Alī and spoke critically of 'Uthmān.[2] Such men came to form an important element of the nucleus of 'Alī's followers (*shī'ah*) and to champion the cause of the Prophet's family (*ahl al-bayt*).

The Shī'ī alternative to the institution of the caliphate is explicitly enunciated, perhaps for the first time, against the rule of 'Uthmān and his Umayyad cohorts. Ya'qūbī reports that when 'Uthmān was finally declared Caliph in the Prophet's Mosque, a man saw Miqdād b. al-Aswad, one of 'Alī's chief supporters, sitting there and visibly troubled. Miqdād said:

> I marvel at the people of the Quraysh and how they continue to block the people of the household of their Prophet from attaining to this office, though among them [the latter] there is a man who was the first to accept

2. al-Ya'qūbī, vol. 2, pp. 162–163.

> faith, and he is the cousin of the Messenger of God. He is the most learned of men and the best informed in the religion of God. He is the man of the greatest feats in Islam; the man with the greatest insight into the right course; the man who is most capable of guiding men to the straight way.

Miqdād then enumerated some of ʿAlī's most significant epithets as the imām of the Muslims, anticipating the viewpoint of the future Shīʿī doctrine of the imamate: "By God, they have precluded him from it [the caliphate] – he who guides aright (*al-hādī*), he who is rightly guided (*al-muhtadī*), the pure and unblemished (*al-ṭāhir al-naqī*) man." Yaʿqūbī no doubt intended by this account to demonstrate wide support for ʿAlī's imamate. He thus goes on to report that the man left Miqdād and went next to Abū Dharr, another one of ʿAlī's noted supporters, and related to him what Miqdād had said. Abū Dharr concurred saying, "My brother Miqdād surely tells the truth." The man finally went to ʿAbd Allāh b. Masʿūd, a well-known Companion and traditionist, and told him. Ibn Masʿūd said, "We were indeed forewarned, but we did not heed the warning."[3]

ʿAlī's attitude towards ʿUthmān's *bayʿah* and his conviction of the legitimacy of his own claim to the leadership of the Muslim community is best expressed in his response to ʿAbd al-Raḥmān's demand that all the men of the *shūrā* council delegate to him (ʿAbd al-Raḥmān) the matter of choosing a successor to ʿUmar. ʿAlī said:

> All praise be to God who sent Muḥammad from among us [the house of Hāshim] as a prophet and messenger. For, we are the house of prophethood, the essence of wisdom, the safe haven of the inhabitants of the earth and the means of salvation for those who seek it. Ours is the right [to the imamate] whether we are granted it and decide to accept it, or whether we are denied it. No one will ever precede me in calling others to the truth, or in acting kindly towards a next-of-kin.[4]

This discourse contains all the major elements of the Shīʿī doctrine of the imamate. It also clearly indicates that this doctrine began to be formulated, at least in part, as a reaction to ʿUthmān's rule and the radical

3. Ibid.
4. al-Ṭabarī, vol. 4, p. 236.

changes it brought to the Muslim community, and to its social, religious, and political institutions, and its customs. It is to some of these changes that we shall now turn.

'Uthmān is depicted by most historians as a man of deep piety and mild and generous disposition. He was among the early Companions who accepted Islam in Makkah. He was twice son-in-law of the Prophet, and one of the Immigrants to Abyssinia.[5] In the course of enumerating the virtues of the Companions, Ibn 'Abbās is said to have described 'Uthmān as a noble and pious man who spent his nights in prayer, and was eager in the performance of good deeds.[6]

In the early years of his caliphate, 'Uthmān was, according to most historians, a prudent and magnanimous ruler who practiced leniency towards the people and fairness in the distribution of wealth. Ṭabarī quotes a letter that 'Uthmān addressed to all his governors immediately after his accession to the caliphate. This letter, if authentic, attests to the high idealism with which 'Uthmān, at the start of his caliphate, viewed his role as the imām of the Muslims. He asserts that the imāms, or rulers of the Muslim community, are charged by God to be "shepherds of the people, and not tax collectors." 'Uthmān then admonishes his governors to observe strict justice in managing the affairs of both Muslims and non-Muslims in their domains, and to deal justly even with their enemies.[7]

However sincere in upholding such lofty principles, 'Uthmān was unable to maintain them. During his reign, we are told, many Companions became exceedingly wealthy. They built large and luxurious mansions, kept numerous slaves, owned much livestock, and amassed great wealth. Mas'ūdī contrasts this new state of affairs with the austere and harsh rule of 'Uthmān's predecessor: "This was not the case during the time of 'Umar b. al-Khaṭṭāb. Rather it was then a clear and straight way." By way of illustrating this point, Mas'ūdī reports

5. See Muḥammad Ibn Sa'd, *al-Ṭabaqāt al-kubrā*, 9 vols. (Beirut: Dār Ṣādir, n.d.), vol. 1, p. 55.
6. al-Mas'ūdī, vol. 3, pp. 244–245. See also al-Balādhurī, vol. 2, pp. 487–248.
7. al-Ṭabarī, vol. 4, pp. 244–245. This letter is quoted in full in Appendix I.

that 'Umar and his son 'Abd Allāh spent sixteen dinars on their *ḥajj* pilgrimage. 'Umar reproachfully observed, "We were wasteful on this journey."[8]

'Uthmān was probably fully conscious of the contrast between himself and his predecessor. But, it is doubtful whether he could have done anything to mitigate the social disparity between poor and rich, as it was a natural consequence of the community's growth into a vast Muslim empire. In any case, he appears to have tried to emulate 'Umar's harshness rather than his austerity or strict justice.

Two interconnected factors worked against 'Uthmān. They were his weak and indecisive personality, due in part to his advanced age, and his intriguing and ambitious Umayyad relatives.[9] 'Uthmān inherited from 'Umar a functioning, highly motivated, and prosperous social and military administration. In the face of such prosperity, it was virtually impossible for the aged Caliph to restrain the ambitious men of the Quraysh, and especially the Umayyads and their allies, from seeking power and wealth by all conceivable means. To this end, the shaykh of the Banū Umayyah as well as his venerable office were manipulated by his crafty and self-interested kinsmen.

Perhaps to compensate for the gradual loss of the moral and religious character of the caliphal office, 'Uthmān increasingly stressed the power, rather than the moral persuasion, of the caliph, and the duty of the people to render him absolute obedience. Seeking to justify some of his serious departures from the conduct of the first two caliphs, 'Uthmān asserted, "Abū Bakr and 'Umar decided with regard to this public wealth to observe frugality towards themselves and their families. But I have decided to be generous towards my next-of-kin."[10] In his effort to forestall any criticism of this policy, 'Uthmān reminded a

8. al-Mas'ūdī, vol. 3, p. 77.
9. 'Uthmān was probably born around 574 C.E. and died around the age of 82–86. This means that he was at least seventy years old when he assumed the caliphate. See Ibn Khalīfah b. Khayyāṭ al-'Uṣfurī, *Ta'rīkh Khalīfah bin Khayyāṭ*, ed. Suhayl Zakkār, 2 vols. (Cairo: Wizārat al-Irshād al-Qawmī, n.d.), vol. 1, p. 192.
10. al-Balādhurī, vol. 2, p. 512.

disaffected assembly of the men of Madīnah of their duty to obey "those in authority over them" (see Q.4:59). He continued, "Fear God your Lord, therefore, and know that the prerogative of the caliphate is a grave matter, far greater than you think."[11]

In A.H. 26, only two years after his accession to the caliphate, 'Uthmān had his first serious confrontation with his subjects. It was over his decision to enlarge the sacred Mosque of the Ka'bah, and the refusal of some people to sell their houses to be demolished and incorporated into the Mosque. 'Uthmān seized the houses by force and put their purchase price into the central treasury. The people rose up in protest, and 'Uthmān ordered them to prison, saying, "It is only my clemency that gave you the audacity to rise up against me. 'Umar dealt in the same way with you, but you did not dare raise your voices before him."[12]

In addition to this confrontation, historians present a long list of grievances that the people held against 'Uthmān, indicating a serious break with the moral and social tradition of the Prophet's Companions, and a violation of the sanctity with which the two venerable shaykhs had surrounded the office of the vicegerency (*khilāfah*) of the Messenger of God. 'Uthmān was faulted for rehabilitating his uncle al-Ḥakam b. Abī al-'Aṣ, who was banished from Madīnah by the Prophet, and whom neither Abū Bakr nor 'Umar had pardoned.[13] 'Uthmān justified the rehabilitation on the ground that he had interceded for al-Ḥakam with the Prophet shortly before the Prophet's death, and that the Prophet had in fact promised to pardon him and allow him and his family to return to Madīnah.[14] 'Uthmān also granted al-Ḥakam's son, Marwān, the fifth of all the revenues of the province

11. al-Kūfī, vol. 2, p. 152.
12. Ibid., p. 151; see also al-Ya'qūbī, vol. 2, p. 164.
13. Al-Ḥakam accepted Islam only on the day of the conquest of Makkah. He is reported to have mocked the Prophet and spied on him while he was with one of his wives. Thus the Prophet banished Al-Ḥakam and his family from Madīnah to al-Ṭā'if and died without pardoning him. See Ibn Ḥajar, vol. 1, pp. 345–346.
14. See al-Balādhurī, vol. 2, pp. 513–514.

of Africa. This act was criticized on the ground that the Qur'ān clearly stipulates that the fifth of any kind of booty belongs to "God, His Messenger, the next-of-kin, the orphans and the destitute" (Q.8:48).

The elders of the Immigrants and Supporters also objected to 'Uthmān's lavish mansions, of which he built seven for his wives and daughters, as well as to the palaces that Marwān built with his ill-gained African wealth.[15] Moreover, 'Uthmān ordered the collector of the alms of the merchants of the Madīnah market to turn over the accumulated wealth to al-Ḥakam. The man refused and 'Uthmān reprimanded him, saying, "You are only our treasurer. If, therefore, we favor you with any thing, then accept it gratefully; but if we leave you alone, then keep silent." The man objected, "I am not your or your family's treasurer; I am the treasurer of the Muslims." He then angrily threw the keys of the treasury to the assembled Muslims while 'Uthmān was delivering the Friday prayer sermon.[16]

The people further objected to 'Uthmān's flagrant disregard of the right of the Immigrants and Supporters to their proper share of wealth and power in an ever-expanding and prosperous state. He appointed his own relatives, without any consideration of age or experience, to high and lucrative administrative posts. 'Uthmān also distributed lands among certain people of Madīnah who were not Companions, nor had they participated in the military expeditions of the Muslims. He likewise enclosed large plots of common pasture lands for his own private use.[17]

Another breach of the tradition of his predecessors was 'Uthmān's dismissal of the pious and peaceful Companion Sa'd b. Abī Waqqāṣ, who was appointed governor of Kūfah by 'Umar, and his appointment of his own half brother, al-Walīd b. 'Uqbah. Surprised by al-Walīd's sudden appearance in Kūfah, Sa'd asked, "Are you coming as a

15. Ibn Qutaybah, vol. 1, p. 50.
16. al-Kūfī, vol. 2, pp. 168–169. al-Balādhurī reports two similar incidents, one with Ibn Mas'ūd and the other with 'Abd Allāh b. al-Arqam, two well-known Companions who served as 'Uthmān's treasurers. See al-Balādhurī, vol. 2, pp. 518 and 547.
17. Ibn Qutaybah, vol. 1, p. 50. See also al-Balādhurī, vol. 2, p. 526.

governor [*amīr*] or a visitor?" "No, but as a governor," al-Walīd answered. Sa'd wondered, "I do not know, have I become foolish after you?" Al-Walīd replied, "You have not become foolish after me, nor have I become a better man after you. Rather, these people have attained dominion and thus are keeping it for themselves."[18]

Even more serious, from the point of view of the sacred law (*sharī'ah*) of Islam, was 'Uthmān's refusal to apply the maximum punishment (*ḥadd*) against al-Walīd after he led the morning prayers at the main mosque of Kūfah drunk. Al-Walīd's wanton drunkenness and total disregard for the religious and social demands of his office led one of the pious men of Kūfah to observe, "'Uthmān has sought to honor his brother at the price of disgracing the community of Muḥammad."[19] Only when the people of Kūfah, who were known for their anti-Umayyad sentiments and 'Alid sympathies, threatened rebellion, did 'Uthmān dismiss al-Walīd and appoint another Umayyad governor. This was another of his kinsmen, Sa'īd b. al-'Aṣ, who was a more sober and experienced administrator, but no more popular than his predecessor.[20]

The men of the Immigrants and Supporters angrily blamed 'Abd al-Raḥmān b. 'Awf for 'Uthmān's unconscionable behavior. Ibn 'Awf reproached 'Uthmān, saying, "I brought you to the fore on condition that you deal with us in accordance with the practice of Abū Bakr and 'Umar. Yet you contradict them and favor your kinsmen and set them over the necks of the Muslims." 'Uthmān answered, "'Umar deprived his next-of-kin for the sake of God, and I bestow generous gifts on my next-of-kin also for the sake of God." 'Abd al-Raḥmān angrily retorted, "I call God to witness that I will never speak to you henceforth." Thus, when 'Uthmān went to visit him on his deathbed, Ibn 'Awf turned his face to the wall and refused to speak to him.[21]

18. al-Balādhurī, vol. 2, p. 516.
19. Ibid., p. 520; see also p. 521.
20. See al-Ya'qūbī, vol. 2, p. 165.
21. Ibn 'Abd Rabbih al-Andalusī, *al-'Iqd al-farīd*, 8 vols. (Beirut: Dār al-Fikr, n.d.), vol. 5, p. 33.

'Uthmān's Critics: 'Ammār b. Yāsir and Abū Dharr al-Ghifārī

We have already noted 'Alī's strong opposition and the emergence of a clearly identifiable party (*shī'ah*) of 'Alī's followers offering a well-articulated alternative to 'Uthmān's rule. Prominent among 'Alī's supporters were two Companions of the Prophet, 'Ammār b. Yāsir and Abū Dharr al-Ghifārī. Both were uncompromising in their demands for egalitarian justice and moral probity. 'Uthmān alienated 'Alī and his supporters among the Companions and the general populace by inflicting personal harm on both men. 'Ammār was severely beaten by 'Uthmān, Marwān b. al-Ḥakam and other Umayyad men, and left unconscious at the door of the Mosque. This because 'Ammār was deputed by a group of Immigrants and Supporters to carry an open letter to 'Uthmān recounting all his deviations from the norms set by Abū Bakr and 'Umar, and urging him to mend his ways.[22]

The case of the other Companion, Abū Dharr, is highly indicative of the intensifying socio-economic and religious rift in Muslim society. Historians, however, are deeply divided regarding the nature and extent of the conflict between 'Uthmān and Abū Dharr, and hence, between the political establishment and an increasingly vocal opposition. In themselves, the writings of Muslim historians reflect the future development of this rift into a profound split in the Muslim community. We shall take, for example, the interpretations of Ya'qūbī and Ṭabarī.

Ya'qūbī presents the conflict as one between the *shī'ah* of 'Alī and the rest of the Muslim community. In his exposition, the point at issue for Abū Dharr was not simply 'Uthmān's nepotism and his deviation from the normative conduct of the two shaykhs, but more importantly, the determination of the men of the Quraysh to deny Muḥammad's family their legitimate right to the spiritual and temporal leadership of his community.

Abū Dharr is said to have expounded daily at the Prophet's Mosque, proclaiming the excellences of Muḥammad and his family

22. al-Balādhurī, vol. 2, pp. 537–541, esp. p. 539.

(*ahl al-bayt*) and reproaching the Muslims for not recognizing those excellences. The words that Ya'qūbī attributes to Abū Dharr, if authentic, are significant, as they express both in idiom and concept the Shī'ī doctrine of the imamate. Abū Dharr began by asserting that God favored the prophets Adam, Noah, and Abraham and his descendants over the rest of humankind (Q.3:33). He further asserted that among all the prophets and their descendants Muḥammad was the first in rank and most highly favored by God. His descendants were, moreover, the true guides to the truth. Abū Dharr continued:

> They are among us as the heaven above and the Ka'bah with its curtains; they are a high beacon. They are as the sun in its zenith, the full moon, and the guiding star [see Q.16:16]. They are as the olive tree whose oil shines forth and whose fruit is blessed [see Q.24:35].

Abū Dharr went on to declare that Muḥammad was heir to the knowledge and high status of Adam and all the prophets after him, and that 'Alī was the vicegerent (*waṣī*) and heir to Muḥammad. He then reproached his fellow Muslims, saying:

> You are a community that has fallen into confusion after its Prophet. Had you brought to the fore those whom God placed ahead and placed back those whom God placed behind, and had you confirmed authority [*walāyah*] and [prophetic] inheritance in the people of the house of your Prophet, you would have been abundantly blessed.[23] Then the intimate friend [*walī*] of God ['Alī] would not have been troubled with care. No aim of the obligations [*farā'iḍ*] given by God would have gone unfulfilled. Nor would any two men have differed concerning a precept of God, but that you would have found right knowledge with them [the Prophet's family, *ahl al-bayt*], deduced from the Book of God and the *sunnah* of his prophet.[24]

According to this account, 'Uthmān exiled Abū Dharr to Syria, where he continued to castigate 'Uthmān at the mosque in Damascus before a growing and attentive audience. This led Mu'āwiyah, the Caliph's cousin and governor of Syria, to ask 'Uthmān to recall Abū

23. Literally: ". . . you would have eaten from above your heads and beneath your feet." See Q.5:66.
24. al-Ya'qūbī, vol. 2, p. 171.

Dharr before he incited the people against both of them. Ibn A'tham al-Kūfī, on the other hand, reports that Abū Dharr was in Damascus when he heard of 'Ammār's treatment at the hands of 'Uthmān and his relatives, and it was only then that he began to angrily censure 'Uthmān at the main mosque of the city. Both historians agree, however, that 'Uthmān instructed Mu'āwiyah to send Abū Dharr to him on a camel without saddle and to have his escort treat him harshly. Thus Abū Dharr arrived in Madīnah exhausted and with his legs lacerated from constant travel.[25]

Abū Dharr is reported to have accused 'Uthmān and his Umayyad kinsmen of usurping God's wealth and authority. This imprudent behavior, Abū Dharr asserted, had been predicted and denounced by the Prophet, who said: "When the number of the sons of Umayyah shall reach thirty men, they shall take God's wealth as a commodity to be circulated among them, His servants as their personal slaves, and His religion as an object of perfidy and corruption."[26]

Ṭabarī's account of Abū Dharr's confrontation with the caliphal establishment has a completely different emphasis. He aims at discrediting Abū Dharr and the pro-'Alid opposition movement associated with him, as well as exonerating 'Uthmān from any wrongdoing. He thus links Abū Dharr to a probably fictitious character called 'Abd Allāh ibn Saba', also known as Ibn al-Sawdā'. Ibn Saba' is said to have been a Yamanite Jew who was credited with being the founder of extremist Shi'ism.[27] Ṭabarī, however, admits that his account – which he relates on the authority of Sayf b. 'Umar, himself an enigmatic figure – is only one of many that he did not wish to mention because he thought them too shameful.

25. Ibid., pp. 171–172; al-Kūfī, vol. 2, p. 155. Al-Balādhurī (vol. 2, p. 543 and pp. 541–546) also corroborates this account.
26. al-Ya'qūbī, vol. 2, p. 172.
27. On the role and personality of 'Abd Allāh b. Saba', see Murtaḍā al-'Askarī, *'Abd Allāh Ibn Saba' wa-asāṭīr ukhrā*, (Baghdad: Kulliyat Uṣūl al-Dīn, 1388/1968), pp. 25–60; and, 'Abd Allāh Fayyāḍ, *Tārīkh al-imāmiyyah wa-aslāfihim min al-shī'ah mundh nash'at al-tashayyu' ḥattā Maṭla' al-qarn al-rābi' al-hijrī*, 2nd. edn. (Beirut: Mu'assasat al-A'lamī, 1395/1975), pp. 92–110.

Abū Dharr, Ṭabarī tells us, met Ibn al-Sawdā' who said to him: "Do you not marvel, O Abū Dharr, at Mu'āwiyah's saying 'All wealth is God's wealth'? Do not all things belong to God? But he seems to wish to arrogate to himself wealth without giving the Muslims their due share." Abū Dharr, who was in Damascus, went to Mu'āwiyah and reprimanded him, and the latter admitted that wealth belonged to God and the Muslims. Then two Companions, 'Ubādah b. al-Ṣāmit and Abū al-Dardā', brought forward Ibn al-Sawdā', whom they accused of having incited Abū Dharr against Mu'āwiyah. Abū al-Dardā' then turned to Ibn al-Sawdā' and said, "I think that you are a Jew."[28]

Having identified Abū Dharr with an extremist fringe movement, Ṭabarī goes on to accuse him of fomenting trouble by inciting the poor in Damascus against the rich. Abū Dharr, Ṭabarī reports, used to repeat the Qur'ānic reproach: "Announce to those who hoard gold and silver and do not spend it in God's cause, that they shall have a painful torment, on a day when it will be heated in the fire of Hell, wherewith their foreheads, sides and backs will be seared" (Q.9:34–35).[29] Perceiving the danger of Abū Dharr's activities, Mu'āwiyah wrote to 'Uthmān to warn him of the consequences. 'Uthmān answered, "Sedition is about to raise its head; do not, therefore, open festering wounds!"[30] 'Uthmān then asked Mu'āwiyah to send Abū Dharr to him with good provisions and an able guide, and to deal with him kindly.

Abū Dharr repeated to 'Uthmān the admonition he had given to Mu'āwiyah and added that men should not accumulate abundant wealth. 'Uthmān replied that he could only counsel frugality and prudence, but could not force people to adopt austerity. Abū Dharr then asked permission to depart Madīnah, as the Prophet had ordered him to do so "when wealth and luxurious houses multiply." 'Uthmān advised Abū Dharr to obey the Prophet's directive, whereupon Abū Dharr chose self-exile to al-Rabadhah, an isolated spot between Makkah and Madīnah. 'Uthmān gave Abū Dharr a good number of camels and two

28. al-Ṭabarī, vol. 4, p. 283.
29. Ibid.
30. Ibid., pp. 283–284.

slaves. He also counselled him not to sever his relations with Madīnah, so that he would not revert to his former nomadism.

In this account Ṭabarī not only wishes to exonerate 'Uthmān from wrongdoing and to discredit extremist protest movements, he also consciously seeks to play down the idea of any deep rift or disagreement among the Prophet's Companions. He thus adduces a report from the famous traditionist, Ibn Sīrīn, who asserted that Abū Dharr "voluntarily went to settle in al-Rabadhah because he saw that 'Uthmān would not agree with him." Ṭabarī also relates that the Prophet said to Abū Dharr, "Hear and obey, even if the man in authority over you is a lowly slave with a mutilated nose."[31]

It was suggested above that Abū Dharr's opposition illustrates a deep and growing conflict between the socio-economic and political aristocracy of the Quraysh, specifically the Umayyad clan represented by 'Uthmān, and an underprivileged group of considerable size and influence. This group, which consisted largely of the Anṣār of Madīnah and other non-Qurayshite elements, found in 'Alī b. Abī Ṭālib a champion and guide. That the group also included some notable Companions no doubt added greatly to its prestige and credibility, and is probably the reason that the conflict has been cast by historians in a primarily religious framework.

'Uthmān and the Clash between Religious Authority and Political Power

Religion and politics in Islam are ideally two sides of a single and all-inclusive framework or way of life. Within this framework, politics, both in theory and practice, ought to be an aspect of the Islamic *sharī'ah*, or sacred law. The *sharī'ah*, moreover, is a moral and religious system whose purpose is to inculcate certain moral imperatives; safeguard the general welfare (*maṣlaḥah*) of both the individual and society; and, regulate Divine-human relationship through proper worship and righteous living.

31. Ibid., pp. 284–285.

A proper and harmonious functioning of the religious and political aspects of this system requires total obedience to Divine authority and its human agents here on earth. This principle of obedience is categorically expressed in the Qur'ānic dictum "O you who have faith, obey God and obey the Messenger and those of you who are in authority" (Q.4:59). Obedience to God here means fulfilling His religious and moral obligations (*farā'iḍ*), endeavoring to approximate God's justice and mercy by avoiding wrongdoing and oppression, and performing righteous works. This fundamental principle is expressed in the Qur'ānic moral injunction of commanding that which is good, decent, or morally acceptable (*ma'rūf*) and forbidding that which is evil, indecent, or morally reprehensible (*munkar*).[32] Obedience to the Messenger means following his way or example (*sunnah*) in fulfilling the Divine obligations and injunctions. Obedience to those in authority means obedience with the intention of achieving the proper conditions and circumstances conducive to obedience to God and His Messenger. This demands that those in authority themselves set an example of unwavering obedience to God and His Messenger.

'Uthmān, as we have seen, laid increasing stress on obedience to those in authority, but did not himself feel obligated to abide by the conditions on which such obedience was founded. In this he set a precedent – the ruler's power rose above the principles of justice and moral uprightness that caliphal authority was predicated on. 'Uthmān in the end lost his moral authority, and with it his life. This was because he could not, while most of the Companions were still alive, retain his political, social, and economic control without the religious and moral framework.

'Uthmān's loss of moral and political authority happened gradually as Umayyad men exercised power and engaged in intrigue with increasing impunity. The turning point in 'Uthmān's tragic career probably arrived midway in his caliphate. Ṭabarī reports an anecdote

32. Commanding the good and forbidding evil (*al-amr bil-ma'rūf wal-nahī 'ann al-munkar*) is an oft-repeated injunction in the Qur'ān. See for examples 3:104, 110, 114; 7:157; 9:71; 22:41; 31:17.

that symbolically signifies his loss of authority. In the sixth year of his twelve-year rule, the ring of the Prophet fell off 'Uthmān's finger into a well outside Madīnah and was never found.[33]

'Uthmān's rule remains one of the most controversial political issues for Muslim historians who, for the most part, filter it through personal interpretations and points of view rather than presenting impartial historical narrative. This is true not only of Muslim historians, but of Western classical orientalists as well.[34] Be that as it may, 'Uthmān's policies reawakened deep-seated tribal hostilities between Hashimites and Umayyads. They brought into sharp conflict the axiom of obedience to the imām or leader of the Muslims and the principle of justice on which this religio-political authority ultimately rests. 'Uthmān's rule, moreover, set an unfortunate precedent of family control over all affairs of the state and its wealth, power, and social and political life. This unchecked exercise of power over the Muslim community brought to the fore old animosities between the two principle houses of the Quraysh.

Hostilities between the sons of Umayyah and Hāshim went back to pre-Islamic times, when the two houses vied with one another for the guardianship of the Ka'bah and the power and prestige that this high office entailed. It should therefore come as no surprise that Muḥammad's message was initially opposed by the Banū Umayyah and their allies, who could not but anticipate that Muḥammad's prophethood would substantiate his clan's claim to political supremacy. Thus, many of their notables did not join the new community or profess its faith until the surrender of Makkah left them no recourse. With 'Uthmān, the Umayyads established a dynasty that was to rule the growing Muslim state for over a century.

'Alī's brief caliphate, following 'Uthmān's brutal assassination, was only a short interruption of Umayyad rule. It was, moreover, fraught with conflict, intrigue, and bloody civil strife. The nature and purpose

33. al-Ṭabarī, vol. 4, p. 231.

34. A significant departure from a clearly pro-Umayyad stance is Madelung's already cited work, *The Succession to Muḥammad*; see in this regard pp. 78–140.

of this struggle is vividly depicted in a brief exchange that allegedly took place between Abū Sufyān and 'Uthmān, immediately after the latter's accession to power. Abū Sufyān counselled:

> The caliphate has finally come to you after the men of Taym [Abū Bakr] and 'Adī ['Umar]. Manipulate it therefore as you would a ball, and let its pillars be the sons of Umayyah. It is only kingship (*mulk*) that is at issue, for I know not what Paradise is, or Hell.[35]

As for caliphal authority and its moral framework, 'Uthmān chose to rest his power not on his own status as an old and venerable companion of the Prophet, nor on the moral and religious character of his office, but on the military might, political power, and intrigues of his Umayyad governors. In one of his sharp confrontations with the Immigrants and Supporters, 'Uthmān is said to have threatened: "By God, I surely command a far greater number of supporters than did the son of al-Khaṭṭāb, and I am of greater power." The problem at issue was 'Uthmān's large monitory gifts to his Umayyad relatives, which he justified on the grounds that they came from surplus wealth and did not deprive anyone of his proper share: "Do you not have each his rightful share of the wealth? Why then can I not do with the surplus whatever I wish? Otherwise, why am I the leader (*imām*)?"[36]

'Uthmān's threat was reinforced by Mu'āwiyah's warning to the Companions to beware the might of his Syrian armies. He said, "I commend my elder (*shaykh*) to you that you treat him well. By God, if he were killed among you, I would fill the city with horses and men against you." That Mu'āwiyah could make good his threat was beyond any doubt, as he controlled a well-disciplined and well-paid loyal army. Addressing 'Ammār b. Yāsir, 'Uthmān's inveterate critic, Mu'āwiyah continued:

> There are in Syria one hundred thousand horsemen, and twice that number of their sons and allies, all receiving their regular pay. These men do not know 'Alī and his close kinship [to the Prophet], or 'Ammār and

35. al-Maqrīzī, pp. 18–19.
36. Ibn Qutaybah, vol. 1, p. 46.

> his priority [in accepting Islam]. Nor do they care about al-Zubayr and his Companionship, or Ṭalḥah and his migration [with the Prophet]. Nor do they fear Ibn 'Awf and his wealth, or Sa'd b. Abī Waqqāṣ and the efficacy of his prayer.[37]

In the end, 'Uthmān's trust in the loyalty of his kinsmen was misplaced; they used their power to defend not their venerable elder, but their own interests. They regarded themselves not as functionaries of a state, representing the moral, political, and economic interests of the Muslim community, but as feudal landlords and rulers in their own right. This attitude is well typified in a provocative remark that Sa'īd b. al-'Āṣ, 'Uthmān's governor of Kūfah, made in the presence of some of 'Alī's staunchest supporters: "Certainly this Sawād [that is the rich agricultural lands of the two Rivers] is a garden for the people of the Quraysh." Incensed by this remark, Mālik al-Ashtar, a Yamanite resident of Kūfah and close confident of 'Alī, challenged him, saying, "You mean that this Sawād, which God has granted us through our own swords, is a garden for you and your people? By God, no share that any of you shall have of it will ever exceed that of any of us."[38]

'Uthmān's answer to any expression of discontent was to deport the alleged instigators, most often to Syria for Mu'āwiyah to deal with. For the most part, such instigators were among 'Alī's followers. This, of course, deepened the antagonism between Umayyads and Hashimites, and between the Quraysh and other Arab tribes and their clients. It, moreover, initiated one of the deepest schisms in Islam by polarizing Muslims into partisans of 'Alī and 'Uthmān, and of Hashimites and Umayyads. Some of the consequences of this polarization were, first, to compromise justice for authority and order; second, to create sects and schools of thought that were to long outlast the conflict itself; and finally, to cause much civil strife, bloodshed and tragedy in the Muslim community. 'Uthmān himself was the first victim of this unfortunate process.

37. Ibid., p. 32. It is interesting that, aside from 'Ammār, the men mentioned here had constituted the *shūra* council.

38. al-Ṭabarī, vol. 4, p. 319. See also al-Kūfī, vol. 2, pp. 171–172.

Following the sharp encounter between the men of Kūfah and Sa'īd b. al-'Āṣ over the Sawād, the people rebelled and 'Uthmān was forced to dismiss him and appoint instead Abū Mūsā al-Ash'arī, a well-known Companion of the tribe of Qays of the Yaman. Abū Mūsā was a respected man, but of weak and indecisive personality. Like many Companions, he feared sedition and was willing to sacrifice anything, including the principles of justice and moral integrity, for unity and order. At the time of Abū Mūsa, 'Uthmān's third appointee to the governorshp of Kūfah, the Caliph's inequitable and nepotistic policies were widely discussed, and calls for his deposition were openly voiced. This was in fact the sentiment of the Kufans whom Abū Mūsā attempted to mollify, but with little success. He addressed the angry mob, saying, "O men, hold your peace! I heard the messenger of God say: 'Anyone who rises up in rebellion when the people have an imām' – and by God, he did not say a just imām – 'seeking thereby to create sedition and disunity, you must kill him.'"[39]

The forcible expulsion of Sa'īd b. al-'Āṣ by the Kufans, as well as the disaffection of the inhabitants of other cities with their governors, prompted 'Uthmān to gather all his governors for consultation. Some advised him to occupy the people with wars and conquests. Others suggested that he confirm them in their posts and act decisively against the opposition, by killing its leaders if necessary. His notorious governor of Egypt, 'Abd Allāh b. Abī Sarḥ, advised 'Uthmān to use the wealth of the central treasury to buy the people's loyalty. 'Amr b. al-'Āṣ, whom 'Uthmān had dismissed as governor of Egypt in favor of Ibn Abī Sarḥ, objected, "I see that you have imposed upon the people things that they dislike. You must therefore decide to act justly, but if you will not, then you must decide to abdicate." Sensing 'Uthmān's anger, 'Amr justified his harsh words: "I am sure that the people will come to know what each of us has said. I want them to hear of my words, and hence come to trust me. Then would I be able to bring you some good, or at least avert some evil from you." 'Uthmān accepted the

39. al-Ṭabarī, vol. 4, p. 336. See also al-Kūfī, vol. 2, pp. 171–172.

advice of his governors and decided to deprive his opponents of their share of state revenues until they were forced by need to acquiesce.[40]

Following his meeting with his governors, ʿUthmān met privately with Muʿāwiyah to seek his advice on how to deal with an alarmingly growing opposition. Muʿāwiyah suggested that he be allowed to behead ʿAlī, Ṭalḥah, and al-Zubayr. ʿUthmān objected, "Should I kill the Companions of the Messenger of God for no wrong or sin they have committed?" Muʿāwiyah countered, "If you do not kill them, they shall kill you." ʿUthmān insisted that he did not wish be the first successor of the Prophet to shed blood.[41]

Muʿāwiyah then presented ʿUthmān with three alternative courses of action. The first was that he put four thousand Syrian horsemen at ʿUthmān's disposal, for his defense. ʿUthmān rejected this offer because he could not countenance supporting such a large army from the public treasury solely for his own protection. Muʿāwiyah then suggested that all the leaders of the opposition be banished from Madīnah and dispersed far from one another. ʿUthmān, however, did not wish to banish the elders of the Immigrants away from their families. Muʿāwiyah finally requested, "Then, give me authority to demand requital for your blood if you are killed." ʿUthmān assented: "If I am killed, no one shall seek requital for my blood but you."[42]

ʿUthmān was a mild, pious, and generous man, as his responses to Muʿāwiyah suggest. He was, however, unable to rule effectively and became an easy tool in the hands of his unscrupulous kinsmen. It is probable that, towards the end of his caliphate, men like Muʿāwiyah, Marwān b. al-Ḥakam, and ʿAmr b. al-ʿĀṣ came to feel that ʿUthmān had outlived his usefulness and, thus, did nothing to defend him against the rage of his assassins. Some of them may have contributed directly to his tragic death, first by always dissuading him from effecting any real reforms, and second by failing to provide him with adequate protection during his fateful siege.

40. al-Ṭabarī, vol. 4, pp. 330–336.
41. Ibn Qutaybah, vol. 1, p. 49.
42. Ibid.

'Uthmān's behavior, and especially that of his Umayyad governors, became a source of embarrassment to his fellow Companions; many either turned against him, or lost hope of his ever mending his ways. They did not wish the caliphate's dignity to be violated through violence against the Caliph, or its moral norms to be compromised through flagrant deviation. They thus sent 'Alī to speak to 'Uthmān on their behalf. 'Alī reproached 'Uthmān, saying, "The people are all behind me, and they have complained to me concerning you. By God, I do not know what to say to you, for I know nothing that you do not know." He then reminded 'Uthmān of his close relationship to the Prophet, as both Companion and son-in-law. Hence, 'Alī argued, 'Uthmān was more worthy of upholding justice than Abū Bakr and 'Umar had been. He continued:

> Surely the way is straight and clear, and the evident principles of religion are firmly established. You know well that the best of God's servants in His sight is a just imām who is rightly guided, and who guides others aright by upholding a good and accepted custom [*sunnah*] and abolishing a despised innovation [*bid'ah*]. The most wicked of men, therefore, is an oppressive imām who is in error and leads others astray by upholding a despised *bid'ah*, and abolishing a good and accepted *sunnah*.

'Alī then, we are told, warned 'Uthmān:

> Beware that you do not become the killed imām of this community. For, it is predicted that an imām of this community will be killed, which will thus initiate killing and strife in it till the Day of Resurrection. It will fall into utter confusion and will be divided into opposing parties and sects.[43]

Whether these words were put into 'Alī's mouth after the fact, or were actually his prediction of 'Uthmān's tragic fate and its outcome, they describe well the detrimental consequences of 'Uthmān's assassination to subsequent Muslim history.

In the end, 'Uthmān fell victim not only to the personal interests of his unscrupulous kinsmen, but also to those of other important personages in the community. Incensed by 'Uthmān's treatment of 'Ammār b.

43. al-Ṭabarī, vol. 4, p. 337.

Yāsir (who, as we have seen, was beaten and left unconscious at the door of the Mosque) and angered by his decision to make her monetary allowance equal to that of the other wives of the Prophet, ʿĀʾishah incited the people against him. She waved the Prophet's shirt in the Mosque while ʿUthmān was delivering a sermon and exclaimed, "O Muslims, behold the garment of the Messenger of God! It is still not worn out, and yet ʿUthmān has already ruined his *sunnah*. Kill the old man! May God kill the old man."[44]

She is also reported to have unsuccessfully attempted to turn Ibn ʿAbbās against ʿUthmān, saying, "O Ibn ʿAbbās, God has given you good intelligence and understanding. Do not try to prevent the people from killing this tyrant. I know that he will only bring misfortune to his own people as did Abū Sufyān on the day of Badr."[45] But, ʿĀʾishah did find willing allies in Ṭalḥah and al-Zubayr, who appear to have had their own personal ambitions. Yaʿqūbī reports that when ʿUthmān was finally besieged in his house by an angry mob, he called for the keys of the treasury, but they were given to Ṭalḥah instead. Al-Zubayr was ʿĀʾishah's brother-in-law. No wonder then, that these three formed a united force against ʿUthmān.[46]

In desperation, ʿUthmān is reported to have written to Muʿāwiyah to hasten to his rescue. Muʿāwiyah set out with twelve thousand men. He, however, left his men well within Syria and went alone to ʿUthmān who was still under siege. When ʿUthmān asked for the help he had requested, Muʿāwiyah answered that he had first come to find out what was wanted. The Caliph retorted, "No by God, rather you want me to be killed, so that you can claim vengeance for my blood. Go immediately and bring me the men!" Muʿāwiyah left his venerable elder and did not return. Then Marwān begged ʿĀʾishah to intervene, but she refused on the ground that she had already made

44. al-Yaʿqūbī, vol. 2, p. 175; al-Kūfī, vol. 2, p. 225. See also Nabia Abbot, *Aishah the Beloved of Mohammed* (Chicago: University of Chicago Press, 1942 [Repr. New York: Arno Press, 1973]), pp. 108 ff.

45. al-Kūfi, vol. 2, pp. 225–226.

46. al-Yaʿqūbī, vol. 2, p. 175.

preparations for the *ḥajj* pilgrimage. Marwān tried to entice her with money, but to no avail. She angrily exclaimed, "I wish that your fellow were cut up into pieces, and that I could carry him and throw him into the sea."[47]

The Siege and 'Uthmān's Violent Death

Historians do not agree about either the immediate motives behind 'Uthmān's assassination, or the identities of those who carried it out. Ibn Qutaybah reports that the men of Egypt and Kūfah besieged 'Uthmān in response to a letter from the Immigrants calling upon them to exact justice against 'Abd Allāh b. Abī Sarḥ, who was 'Uthmān's governor of Egypt. In this account, the men were led by al-Ashtar, a Kufan supporter and close confident of 'Alī. 'Uthmān finally consented to dismiss ibn Abī Sarḥ and appoint instead Muḥammad b. Abū Bakr, who was 'Alī's devoted step son. Accompanied by a number of Immigrants and Supporters, the new governor was on his way to assume his post when 'Uthmān's servant was caught hastening with a letter bearing his master's seal. The letter ordered ibn Abī Sarḥ to kill Muḥammad b. Abū Bakr and his entourage, and remain in his post. When 'Uthmān was confronted with the letter, he denied any knowledge of it. As a result, the people suspected Marwān b. al-Ḥakam of having forged the letter and demanded that he be questioned and punished. 'Uthmān refused and the siege was intensified.

Although the notables of the Muhājirūn and Anṣār were enraged by what had happened, they provided the besieged Caliph with a good number of bodyguards. Among these were Ḥasan son of 'Alī, 'Abd Allāh b. al-Zubayr, and the famous Companion and traditionist, Abū Hurayrah. As the rumor of the arrival of a large Syrian army come to rescue 'Uthmān spread, the angry rebels became frightened and attempted to set the Caliph's house on fire. When the men inside prepared to fight, 'Uthmān released them from their pledge to defend him because he did not wish to be the cause of bloodshed. In the ensuing

47. Ibid., pp. 175–176.

confusion, a few unknown men among the insurgents forced their way into the house and brutally murdered ʻUthmān.[48]

The early Baṣran historian Khalīfah b. Khayyāṭ (d. 249/854), presents a generally reasonable and concise account of ʻUthmān's assassination. He links the siege of ʻUthmān, and his subsequent death, to the rebellion of his Egyptian subjects. He also adduces the alleged letter of ʻUthmān to his Egyptian governor Ibn Abī Sarḥ, as an immediate cause of this rebellion. He reports that when the leaders of the insurgents discovered ʻUthmān's alleged letter, they returned to Madīnah and complained to ʻAlī, vowing to kill the Caliph. They asked ʻAlī to go with them to confront him, but ʻAlī refused. They angrily protested, "Why then did you write to us [presumably, urging them to rise up against ʻUthmān]?" But ʻAlī categorically denied having written to them. They looked at one another in surprise. Ibn Khayyāṭ's account suggests that such fraudulent letters were forged in the names of ʻAlī, ʻUthmān, and ʻĀ'ishah.[49]

Ibn Khayyāṭ reports that following this meeting with the rebels, ʻAlī left Madīnah. But he immediately adduces a different report asserting that ʻUthmān sent ʻAlī to negotiate with the angry men on his behalf. ʻAlī promised that ʻUthmān would deal with them in accordance with the Book of God and that all their grievances would be redressed. They agreed to lift the siege on five conditions: that banished men be allowed to return their homes; that all those deprived of state stipends be compensated; that war properties (*fay'*) be justly allotted; that all spoils of war be divided equitably; and, their final demand, that ʻUthmān appoint as governors trustworthy and decisive men, and restore ʻAbd Allāh b. ʻĀmir to his post as governor of Baṣrah, and Abū Mūsā to his as governor of Kūfah.[50]

It should be noted that the group besieging ʻUthmān was composed of men with differing tribal, regional, and ideological allegiances.

48. Ibn Qutaybah, vol. 1, pp. 57–58.
49. Ibn Khayyāṭ, vol. 1, pp. 182 and 191–192. See also Ibn ʻAbd Rabbih, vol. 6, pp. 41–43.
50. Ibn Khayyāṭ, vol. 1, pp. 182–183.

The Caliph's sensitivity to this fact is illustrated in the following account. 'Uthmān is reported to have sent for al-Ashtar and asked him what the people wanted from him. Al-Ashtar replied that they insisted that 'Uthmān either relinquish his caliphal authority and let them choose another caliph, or inflict upon himself his due punishment. Or, if he refused to comply, they would kill him. 'Uthmān argued, "I would never remove a garment with which God had clothed me." As for punishing himself, he argued that his frail body would not endure punishment. But if they killed him, he went on, they would never be united in worship, amity, or war against a common foe after him.[51]

The gravity of the act of regicide and the example it could set for subsequent Muslim practice are vividly characterized in a brief interchange between the besieged Caliph and 'Abd Allāh b. 'Umar b. al-Khaṭṭāb. 'Abd Allāh said in amazement, "Do you see what these people are saying? They say 'abandon it [the caliphate] and do not kill yourself.'" He then asked, "If you abandoned it, would you live forever?" "No," 'Uthmān answered. 'Abd Allāh went on, "If you do not abandon it, could they do anything more than kill you?" Again 'Uthmān said no. To Ibn 'Umar's further query as to whether they could guarantee him Paradise or Hell in the hereafter, 'Uthmān's answer was again in the negative. Ibn 'Umar concluded, "I think that you should not take off a garment with which God has clothed you – so that it does not become accepted practice (*sunnah*) – or, whenever people disliked their caliph or imām they would kill him."[52] Although the Caliph took 'Abd Allāh's advice and did not resign, these words were painfully prophetic. The siege of 'Uthmān and the demands for his abdication, followed by his murder, dealt the dignity of the caliphal office a severe blow. This grievous episode forever compromised the authority and even the person of the representative (*khalīfah*) of God and His Messenger. It, moreover, set a precedent by which many later

51. Ibid., p. 182.
52. Ibid., p. 183; see also pp. 183–184.

caliphs were forcibly removed, and sometimes blinded so as to render them legally unfit to rule. Some were even violently murdered.

Like a number of other historians and traditionists, Ibn Khayyāṭ seeks to minimize disagreement amongst the Companions and to safeguard the dignity and legitimacy of 'Uthmān's caliphate. While he does not deny the criticisms and accusations that were levelled against 'Uthmān, they do not, in his view, justify the actions of the insurgents. He therefore presents a number of reports affirming the unwavering support of the Prophet's Companions and their sons, and their willingness to defend the besieged Caliph.

'Uthmān was defenselessly killed, in the view of most historians, not because no one came to his aid, but because he himself preferred death to the shedding of Muslim blood. To the repeated offers made by men of both the Immigrants and the Supporters to fight off the rebellious mob, he said, "I adjure anyone who pledges obedience to me to withhold his hand and arms, for the best of you in my sight is he who withholds his hand and arms." The well-known Companion and Qur'ān compiler, Zayd b. Thābit, is said to have gone to 'Uthmān with a message of support from the Anṣar who stood at the door ready to fight: "If you wish," they said, "we will be God's supporters (*anṣar*) twice." 'Uthmān answered, "I have no need of that, hold your peace!"[53]

Again like most other historians, Ibn Khayyāṭ presents different and conflicting accounts as to who killed 'Uthmān and how the assassination was carried out. He is likewise unclear as to Muḥammad b. Abū Bakr's actual role in 'Uthmān's murder.[54] He reports that the son of Abū Bakr went in to 'Uthmān just before he was killed and sharply rebuked him for his deviation from the practices of his two predecessors. This much seems to be agreed upon by most historians; whether or not he killed the Caliph remains a point of disagreement between them.[55]

53. Ibid., pp. 186–187; see also pp. 188–189.
54. Ibid., pp. 188–189.
55. Ibid., p. 189. See also Ibn 'Abd Rabbih (vol. 6, pp. 36–40) for an interesting account of 'Uthmān's death and Muḥammad b. Abū Bakr's part in it.

Ya'qūbī provides an interesting list of 'Uthmān's murderers. It implicates, amongst others, Muḥammad b. Abū Bakr and Muḥammad b. Abū Ḥudhayfah, both sons of prominent Companions, and 'Amr b. al-Ḥamq al-Khuzā'ī.[56] It is important to note that these men were well-known supporters of 'Alī, who either died fighting in his campaigns, or were slain in his cause.

Ṭabarī presents several disparate accounts of 'Uthmān's murder and the motives behind it. His choice and presentation of reports seem to have been influenced by two major concerns: first, to establish that 'Uthmān was an innocent victim, and then, to lay the blame for the evil act on extremist men and ideas which fall outside the religious and moral value system of Muslim society. To this end, Ṭabarī consciously leaves out accounts that disparage 'Uthmān or any of the Companions, or suggest deep division among them.

In an account reported on the authority of Sayf b. 'Umar, Ṭabarī links 'Uthmān's violent death to 'Abd Allāh b. Saba' and his followers. Ibn Saba' was, we are told, a Yamanite Jew whose mother was a black woman. He accepted Islam during the caliphate of 'Uthmān and thereafter strove tirelessly to lead the Muslims of the Ḥijāz, Irāq, and Syria astray, but without success. He then went to Egypt where he propagated Shī'ī beliefs such as the return (*raj'ah*) from the dead of the followers of the imāms, and their enemies, for the final revenge; 'Alī's vicegerency (*waṣiyyah*) of the Prophet; and, 'Uthmān's unjust usurpation of 'Alī's right to the caliphate. It must be observed that, while the notions of 'Alī's vicegerency and 'Uthmān's usurpation may have been held by some Muslims at the time, it is doubtful whether the Shī'ī doctrine of the *raj'ah* had yet been formulated.

Ṭabarī presents an even closer connection between 'Uthmān's death and the beginning of extremist Shi'ism when he reports, again on the authority of Sayf b. 'Umar, that 'Uthmān sent 'Ammār b. Yāsir with other men to investigate the activities of 'Abd Allāh b. Saba' and his followers. 'Ammār, however, joined the rebellious band in their

56. al-Ya'qūbī, vol. 2, pp. 176–177.

effort to depose 'Uthmān. As the agitators were unable to stir the people against 'Uthmān and his governors, they agreed to use the opportunity of the *ḥajj* pilgrimage as a pretext to invade Madīnah. They were, moreover, joined by a number of 'Alī's Kufan supporters, including al-Ashtar and other notables. The insurgents took Madīnah by surprise and besieged 'Uthmān's house unopposed.

Aiming, no doubt, at presenting a semblance of concord among the Companions, and between them and the inhabitants of the major centers of the Muslim domains, Ṭabarī reports several curious incidents. The people of Egypt were inclined towards 'Alī, those of Baṣrah towards Ṭalḥah, and those of Kūfah towards al-Zubayr. Delegations from the three districts each pressed their champion to seek the caliphate; all three men cursed and rejected them. Furthermore, when the rebels attacked Madīnah and 'Uthmān asked the people of the same areas for military assistance, he received detachments from all of them as well as from Syria. The armies included many Companions and Successors. That these rescuing armies are a pious fiction is obvious, as they played no role in saving the besieged Caliph. Rather, as Ṭabarī also tells us, 'Uthmān was besieged in his house for forty days, while the men of Madīnah were dispersed in their homes and orchards.[57]

In other accounts, Ṭabarī lays the blame for 'Uthmān's death on Marwān b. al-Ḥakam and, to a lesser extent, on Sa'īd b. al-'Aṣ and Mu'āwiyah. He also presents 'Alī as an honest negotiator genuinely concerned for 'Uthmān's life and honor. 'Uthmān is shown to be a vacillating old man who makes promises of reform and repentance, but changes his mind at Marwān's behest. After one such pledge, Marwān swayed 'Uthmān from his resolve and went out to the men who were still surrounding the house, and said: "What do you want that you have gathered as though for a pillage? You have come to take away our kingdom from us. Return to your homes for, by God, we shall never be forced to surrender."[58]

57. al-Ṭabarī, vol. 4, pp. 340–354.
58. Ibid., p. 355; see also pp. 354–365.

Ṭabarī also reports that Marwān counselled 'Uthmān to ask 'Alī to restrain the people until the arrival of Mu'āwiyah's army, at which time the Caliph could revoke his promises. On this advice, 'Uthmān assured 'Alī that he would fulfil his agreement with the people, even if it meant his death. 'Alī replied, "The people would rather have your justice than your life." 'Alī again implored the insurgents to lift their siege, and again they consented, this time on condition that 'Uthmān redress every injustice and that he dismiss any governor they disapproved of. It was agreed that the conditions would be fulfilled within three days in Madīnah, and immediately upon his orders being received in other provinces. But, when the three days had passed and 'Uthmān refused to fulfil his agreement and instead began to make preparations to fight, the insurgents resumed their siege. 'Uthmān argued, "What authority would I have if I dismissed anyone you disliked and appointed anyone you liked? In that case, not I, but you rule."[59]

Before he was murdered, 'Uthmān is said to have pleaded with his assailants, "Do not kill me! For if you do, you will never pray as one congregation after me. Nor will you ever share, as one community, any gains of war after me. For, God will never remove dissension from among you."[60] History bore 'Uthmān out: his death did initiate continuing strife and tragedy, dissension and disunity. But above all, 'Uthmān's rule, and especially his scandalous end, deprived the caliphal office of its normative character and sanctity.

It was observed at the start of this discussion that 'Uthmān's caliphate was a break with tradition. This break has been explained by some contemporary historians simply as the consequence of necessary fiscal and administrative reforms. This is the view of the modern Islamic historian M. A. Sha'bān, who characterizes 'Uthmān's turbulent rule as "the breakdown of the Madinan regime."[61] In his judgment,

59. Ibid., p. 384.
60. Ibid., p. 395.
61. M. A. Shaban, *Islamic History: A New Interpretation*, 2 vols. (Cambridge: Cambridge University Press, 1971), vol. 1, p. 60.

the breakdown happened as a result of the conflict between Makkan and Madinan interests and orientations. 'Uthmān was "Makkan to the core," Sha'bān argues, while 'Alī, who could only remember the Prophet's days of hardship and struggle in Makkah, was Madinan in both interests and support. 'Umar's *shūrā* committee was a Makkan body that failed to see clearly the clash between the interests of the two communities and the necessity, within a large empire, to harmonize those interests.[62]

Sha'bān's "new interpretation" of classical Islamic history is plausible, but only if understood in the context of many religious, social, and economic factors. That 'Uthmān may have wished to change the administration of the Islamic state – from the model of Arab tribal federation to one more suited to a vast multi-ethnic and multicultural empire – does not sufficiently explain the break with tradition and the fracturing of the community. In fact, 'Uthmān was continuing a process that had already begun with 'Umar; it was 'Uthmān's particular manner of effecting the transition, not the change itself, that angered his contemporaries. Perhaps the point is best clarified through a contrasting example, one that shows 'Uthmān working successfully within the overarching religious and social values of the community.

An important aspect of the radical reorganization of the Muslim *ummah* was 'Uthmān's sponsorship of the production of an official rescension (*muṣḥaf*) of the Qur'ān, a procedure that involved the destruction of all other private copies of the sacred Book. Although some Qur'ān bearers and reciters, such as 'Abd Allāh b. Mas'ūd, objected to losing their high status as oral transmitters of a recited Qur'ān, the majority welcomed 'Uthmān's initiative. This was because it protected the text from being obscured behind endless discrepancies, which would have been the result of the unchecked proliferation of different readings. It also unified Muslims around one official and universally accepted text. This was a necessary prerequisite for the development of the religious sciences, particularly jurisprudence.

62. Ibid., pp. 62–63.

6

ʻAlī Waṣī Rasūl Allāh: The Clash of Religion and Politics

Fearing sedition after the murder of ʻUthmān, the people of Madīnah lost no time in choosing ʻAlī as ʻUthmān's successor, as he was the most likely of the surviving candidates of ʻUmar's *shūrā* council. Historians are unanimous in reporting that ʻAlī was chosen by acclamation, and that he insisted on his *bayʻah* taking place in the Mosque, publicly, and with the consent of all the men present.[1] Thus ʻAlī was the first and only popularly elected caliph in Muslim history. However, a number of the notables of the Quraysh had already left Madīnah when the rebellion against ʻUthmān intensified and historians differ widely as to who of the *shūrā* council actually witnessed ʻAlī's *bayʻah*. There is a general consensus among them that Ṭalḥah and al-Zubayr were among the first to pledge allegiance to ʻAlī and assure him of the allegiance of the rest of the Immigrants.[2]

Three Umayyad men were among the few who refused to pledge allegiance: Marwān b. al-Ḥakam, Saʻīd b. al-ʻĀṣ and al-Walīd b. ʻUqbah. Their objections were neither religious nor moral, but were, rather, based on old personal grudges against ʻAlī. They faulted him

1. See al-Ṭabarī, vol. 4, p. 427; al-Masʻūdī, vol. 3, pp. 93–94; al-Yaʻqūbī, vol. 2, p. 178.
2. See for examples, al-Yaʻqūbī, vol. 2, p. 178; Ibn ʻAbd Rabbih, vol. 5, p. 36; and, al-Kūfī, vol. 2, pp. 243–244.

for having killed Sa'īd's father in the battle of Badr, executed al-Walīd's father on the day of the conquest of Makkah, insulted Marwān's father, and finally, for having blamed 'Uthmān for rehabilitating the latter after the Prophet had banished him. The conditions they laid down for giving *bay'ah* were likewise not based on religious or moral considerations; they were matters of personal interest and tribal solidarity. The three men demanded that 'Alī forgive them all their misdeeds, allow them to keep their vast ill-gained wealth, and avenge 'Uthmān's blood. 'Alī's answer, in contrast, reflects his moral and religious idealism: "As for the hurt I caused you, it was not I but the truth that hurt you. As for forgiving you your misdeeds, it is not for me to annul any of God's rights. But, I can assure you that I will deal with you in accordance with the Book of God and the *sunnah* of His Prophet."[3]

Concerning the last condition, different accounts have been reported of 'Alī's attitude towards 'Uthmān's murderers. In the report just cited, 'Alī declared angrily: "If I were to decree their execution today, it would only mean that I would have to do battle with them tomorrow." According to Ibn A'tham al-Kūfī, 'Alī argued: "If I am compelled to kill them now, I should have in fact killed them on that fateful day."[4] Such arguments suggest that 'Alī considered 'Uthmān's death to be an inevitable consequence of the events leading to it and saw the murderers not as identifiable individuals, but rather as a mob of men representing different tribes and regions of the Muslim domains. From this perspective, even if 'Alī had been able to identify 'Uthmān's murderers, punishing them would have involved him in widespread tribal conflict. Be that as it may, the assassination of 'Uthmān was the excuse used to spark the first bloody civil war in Muslim society. Furthermore, it soon became a powerful political and religious event whose theological and juristic implications continue to occupy Muslims.

'Alī's supporters saw his rise to caliphal authority as a victory over

3. al-Ya'qūbī, vol. 2, pp. 178–179.
4. Ibid., vol. 2, p. 179; al-Kūfī, vol. 2, pp. 159–160.

the Quraysh aristocracy and the realization of a just religious cause. This conviction was voiced by Thābit b. Qays b. Shammās on behalf of the Anṣār:

> By God, O Commander of the Faithful, although they preceded you in caliphal authority, they did not surpass you in religion. Your status could never be obscured nor could your high rank be ignored. They all need you in situations of which they have no knowledge, but with your knowledge you are in need of no one.

Speaking for 'Alī's *shī'ah* in Iraq, his faithful warrior and staunch supporter Mālik al-Ashtar went further. He addressed the assembled men, saying, "O people, this is the vicegerent (*waṣī*) of all vicegerents and heir to the knowledge of all the prophets. [This is he] concerning whose faith the Book of God has testified, and to whom the Messenger of God promised the Garden of al-Riḍwān."[5] Such sentiments clearly indicate that 'Alī's supporters believed him to be not simply a political successor (*khalīfah*) to the Prophet, but also his heir (*waṣī*) as the spiritual head (*imām*) of the community. 'Alī himself appears to have considered his caliphal responsibility a Divine trust. He was determined to be just and equitable in all his dealings. As a pre-condition for accepting the caliphal office he declared: "I had no desire to rule over you, but you would not have it otherwise. I now hold no special authority over you, except that I am the keeper of the keys to your public treasury. But I will not take for myself even a small coin [*dirham*] from it above your share. Do you consent?" "Yes," they all replied. 'Alī said, "O God, bear witness over them!"[6]

'Alī wanted to abolish the social stratification that 'Umar had established and 'Uthmān had used to the advantage of his own kinsmen. He not only wished to distribute wealth equally, but also to assign government posts on the basis of personal piety and administrative honesty rather than noble lineage or social prestige. He thus planned to dismiss

5. al-Ya'qūbī, vol. 2, p. 179. Riḍwān is the angelic keeper of Paradise, whose name means "[God's] infinite pleasure."
6. al-Ṭabarī, vol. 4, pp. 427–428.

'Uthmān's governors and to reclaim for the central treasury all the wealth that some had illicitly accumulated during 'Uthmān's rule. His motto was, "You are all God's servants and all wealth is God's wealth, which will be equally divided among you."[7] With regard to those who saw their lineage or priority in Islam as a source of power and high status, his view was: "Anyone who answers the call of God and the Messenger and thus accepts our faith, embraces our religion, and faces our *qiblah* [direction of prayer] is entitled to the rights of Islam, and is subject to its religious and legal punishments (*ḥudūd*)".[8]

In the long run, 'Alī's idealism made him a spiritual and moral example for pious Muslims to emulate; its immediate consequences were anarchy and bloodshed. Al-Mughīrah b. Shu'bah, a shrewd and worldly minded Qurayshite, counselled 'Alī to confirm Mu'āwiyah and all other governors in their posts until he was assured of their loyalty and the loyalty of their armies, and only then to make the changes he wished. 'Alī refused. Seeing that his advice was not heeded, al-Mughīrah returned the next day and advised 'Alī to act decisively with his governors, so that no one would think him weak and ineffectual. Al-Mughīrah is said to have commented, "I gave him good advice but, since he did not heed it, I deceived him."[9]

'Alī's cousin and close confidant 'Abd Allāh Ibn 'Abbās agreed with al-Mughīrah's judgment. He argued that Mu'āwiyah and his Syrian supporters were motivated only by power and wealth and, if 'Alī were to confirm them in their posts, it would be of no consequence to them who succeeded 'Uthmān. But if he dismissed them, they would claim that 'Alī had assumed the caliphal office without proper consultation and would hold him responsible for 'Uthmān's blood. Thus would they incite the people of Syria and Iraq against him. 'Alī countered:

> As for your suggestion that I confirm them in their posts, by God, I have no doubt that this would be good with regard to the transitory life of this

7. Ibn Abī al-Ḥadīd, vol. 4, p. 37.
8. Ibid.
9. al-Ṭabarī, vol. 4, p. 439; see also al-Ya'qūbī, vol. 2, p. 180.

> world and for the proper management of its affairs. But I am obliged by the truth and my knowledge of 'Uthmān's governors to do otherwise; by God, I will never confirm anyone of them.

'Alī concluded, "If they obediently come forward, it will be better for them. But if they should turn away, I would have nothing but the sword for them." In vain Ibn 'Abbās pleaded with him to retire to his orchards in al-Yanbu', far from Madīnah, and wait until the situation calmed down and he secured the loyalty of the general populace. "For," Ibn 'Abbās cautioned, "if you rise today with your supporters against them, they will accuse you tomorrow of 'Uthmān's blood."[10]

This exchange between 'Alī and his pragmatic and prudent cousin indicates that 'Alī was not politically naive, but idealistically intractable. He seems to have realized that his idealism put him on a collision course with a well-established aristocracy animated, not by the old moral and religious ideal of caliphal authority, but by the new socio-political, economic, and military exigencies of a rapidly expanding empire. 'Alī's dilemma was that he could neither leave the community without an imām, nor could he compromise his moral and religious character and status for political expediencies.

Few among 'Alī's fellow Companions shared his idealism, and fewer still agreed with his seemingly unwise reform policies. The case of Ṭalḥah and al-Zubayr is both typical and highly instructive. They are reported to have been among the first Companions to pledge allegiance to 'Alī. They were also the first to revoke it and the first to turn to armed rebellion. Ya'qūbī reports that they complained to 'Alī that they had suffered deprivation after the Prophet. They demanded that 'Alī therefore make them partners in his authority. 'Alī replied, "You are indeed my partners in strength and uprightness and my helpers in times of weakness and incapacity." He then wrote an appointment deed for Ṭalḥah as governor over the Yaman and for al-Zubayr as governor over the districts of Yamāmah and Baḥrayn. But they wanted more and demanded rich gifts from the central treasury as an expression of

10. al-Ṭabarī, vol. 4, pp. 439–440.

"kindness to a near relative."[11] 'Alī angrily rescinded their appointments saying, "But I have shown kindness to you by appointing you trustees over the affairs of the Muslims."[12]

Ibn Qutaybah reports that Ṭalḥah and al-Zubayr asked 'Alī, "Do you know on what condition we pledged allegiance to you?" He answered, "Yes, on condition that you hear and obey, and on that on which you pledged allegiance to Abū Bakr, 'Umar and 'Uthmān." "No," they replied, "but on condition that we be your partners in this affair." Al-Zubayr coveted the governorship of Iraq and Ṭalḥah that of the Yaman. Seeing that 'Alī would not grant them their wishes, they violently turned against him.[13]

According to Ibn Abī al-Ḥadīd, Ṭalḥah and al-Zubayr were encouraged by Mu'āwiyah to rise up against 'Alī and demand revenge for 'Uthmān's death. Mu'āwiyah is reported to have written to al-Zubayr addressing him as "Commander of the Faithful." Having assured al-Zubayr of the allegiance of all the people of Syria to him as caliph, Mu'āwiyah continued: "Hasten therefore to Kūfah and Baṣrah before Ibn Abī Ṭālib precedes you thither, for you will achieve nothing after the loss of these two cities. I have, moreover, pledged allegiance to Ṭalḥah after you. Rise up then with the demand for avenging the blood of 'Uthmān." Ibn Abī al-Ḥadīd observes that this letter was the cause of the hostility of Ṭalḥah and al-Zubayr towards 'Alī.[14]

The Battle of the Camel

Having failed to achieve their objectives by peaceful means, Ṭalḥah and al-Zubayr asked permission of 'Alī to go to Makkah for the lesser pilgrimage (*'umrah*), but in fact they went to organize an insurrection against him. The ensuing conflict, known as the Battle of the Camel,

11. *ṣilat al-raḥim*, literally "strengthening the link with the womb" – meaning a near blood relative – through financial and other kinds of support, is an old Arab social value and a central Qur'ānic doctrine. See for examples: Q.8:75, 33:6 and 47:22.
12. al-Ya'qūbī, vol. 2, pp. 179–180.
13. Ibn Qutaybah, vol. 1, pp. 70–71.
14. Ibn Abī al-Ḥadīd, vol. 1, p. 227.

took place soon after 'Alī gained office.[15] This battle demonstrates the sharp deterioration in the moral and religious conception of the caliphate, and marks the beginning of the triumph of realpolitik over the values on which the Prophet Muḥammad had established the first Islamic commonwealth in Madīnah. Muslims were then motivated by their faith and the promise of Paradise. However, the vast conquests and the rich revenues, which these motivations helped them achieve, tempted many away from their faith and the hereafter, whilst turning others away from the world, including the political life of their own society. The Battle of the Camel was another instance of this shift in values.

We are not concerned in this study with the details of the encounter, but with the key players and their motives in the dramatic events that led to it, as well as the indelible mark it left on subsequent Muslim history. The battle itself was brief, lasting about four hours, yet it claimed the lives of many pious Muslims. It was fought outside the city of Baṣrah in southern Iraq around 'Ā'ishah's camel, hence the designation "Battle of the Camel."

Among the men who lost their lives in this conflict were its two main instigators, Ṭalḥah and al-Zubayr. Ṭalḥah was reported to have been killed by an arrow shot by Marwān b. al-Ḥakam who happened to be present at the time. Marwān exclaimed, "By God, I will not demand revenge for 'Uthmān's blood after this day!" Apparently Marwān held Ṭalḥah to be among those responsible for 'Uthmān's assassination. Ṭalḥah himself is said to have declared as he fell: "I have never seen the life of an elder of the Quraysh so wastefully ended as mine today. For, by God, I never before took a stand on anything but that I knew where I stood except this stand."[16] Observing the fate of his accomplice, Al-Zubayr left the battlefield. He was, however, pursued and killed by a man of the tribe of Tamīm at the incitement of al-Aḥnaf b.

15. 'Uthmān was killed in Dhū al-ḥijjah, in the last month of 35 A.H. The Battle of the Camel took place in Jumādā ii of the following year, 36 (December 656).
16. al-Ya'qūbī, vol. 2, p. 182; see also Ibn Khayyāṭ, vol. 1, p. 200.

Qays, a notable of the Anṣār and one of 'Alī's devoted supporters, who reproached al-Zubayr saying:

> I have never seen a man like this one! He led the inviolable spouse of the Messenger of God out of her sanctuary, violated the sanctity of the curtain which the Messenger of God drew around her in his house, then abandoned her and ran away. Is there no man who would execute God's vengeance upon him?[17]

The wife of the Prophet referred to in this speech is 'Ā'ishah. An examination of the reports concerning her involvement in the uprising help to illustrate some of the issues at stake for the Muslim community. Despite the sense of al-Aḥnaf b. Qays' words, 'Ā'ishah – daughter of Abū Bakr, wife of the Prophet, and "Mother of the Faithful" – was not, as pious tradition has insisted, an unwilling victim of political circumstances. She was, rather, a central character in the dramatic events leading to and following the death of 'Uthmān. First, she called for the death of 'Uthmān, accusing him, as has already been noted, of "ruining the *sunnah* of the Prophet." She then left 'Uthmān besieged in his house, refused to intervene on his behalf with the angry mob, and went to Makkah for the *ḥajj* pilgrimage. But when, on her way back, she learned of 'Alī's accession to the caliphate, she protested, "Why should 'Alī rule over us? I will not enter Madīnah so long as 'Alī holds authority in it."[18]

Another report provides more and interesting details. On her way back to Madīnah, 'Ā'ishah met 'Abd b. Abī Salmā, a distant maternal relative of hers, who informed her of 'Uthmān's death and 'Alī's accession. He related that the people of Madīnah had waited for eight days after 'Uthmān's death before they "all wisely agreed on 'Alī ibn Abī Ṭālib." 'Ā'ishah exclaimed, "Would that the sky had collapsed over the earth before this matter was decided in favor of your fellow. Take me back to Makkah!" She further declared, "By God, 'Uthmān was wrongfully killed! And I will surely demand requital for his blood." Ibn Abī

17. al-Ya'qūbī, vol. 2, p. 183.
18. Ibn Qutaybah, vol. 1, p. 66. See also al-Ya'qūbī, vol. 2, p. 180.

Salmā reminded her that she had been the first to incite the people against 'Uthmān by saying "Kill the old man, for he has rejected faith." She countered that the people, having first made him repent had then wrongfully killed him. "I talked and they talked," she continued, "but my latter speech is better than my former one." The man retorted, "You ordered us to kill the Imām and we obeyed you and killed him. But we believe that his true killer is the one who ordered it."[19]

Two apologetic explanations of 'Ā'ishah's role in the events leading to the tragic Battle of the Camel have been suggested. The first is that she only wished to make peace among the Muslims. The second is that she was an unwilling victim of the political machinations of Ṭalḥah and al-Zubayr. In reality, 'Ā'ishah appears to have had a mind of her own and she was clearly a key player in the opposition. Ṭabarī reports that 'Ā'ishah was in fact a leader among the people, issuing commands and prohibitions and even appointing prayer leaders for them.[20] She also was engaged in negotiations, wrote letters, and gave impassioned speeches inciting people to join her in what she called her effort "to set things right in Muḥammad's community."[21]

In Makkah, 'Ā'ishah had a willing ally in 'Abd Allāh b. 'Āmir, 'Uthmān's governor of the city. She incited the people in the Holy City saying, "[T]his matter will never be resolved so long as this uproar goes on! Exact revenge for 'Uthmān's blood and you will honor Islam." She then commanded, "Rise up therefore concerning this matter and join your brethren of the people of Baṣrah. For, the people of Syria support you; perhaps God will execute vengeance for 'Uthmān and the Muslims."[22]

'Ā'ishah's animosity towards 'Alī originated with the necklace incident, when 'Alī suggested to the Prophet that he divorce her if he had doubts regarding her fidelity.[23] Because of this hostility and 'Ā'ishah's

19. al-Ṭabarī, vol. 4, pp. 458–459.
20. Ibid., vol. 4, p. 450.
21. See Abbot, pp. 149–161.
22. al-Ṭabarī, vol. 4, p. 450.
23. See Abbot, pp. 29–38, and especially p. 33; see also Q.24:11–16.

role in the Battle of the Camel, Shīʿī tradition has championed Umm Salamah, another wife of the Prophet, as a rival to her.

The early Shīʿī historian Yaʿqūbī reports that ʿĀ'ishah went to Umm Salamah to convince her to accompany her to Baṣrah. "Perhaps God may bring peace and harmony into Muḥammad's community at our hands," she argued. Umm Salamah refused, maintaining that it was not for women to meddle with public affairs, but rather, that "the praiseworthy behavior of women is to lower their gaze and observe modesty." She further reprimanded ʿĀ'ishah for violating the rule of seclusion, which the Prophet had imposed on all his wives. ʿĀ'ishah is reported to have been persuaded and to have decided to remain in Makkah, but then Ṭalḥah and al-Zubayr convinced her to accompany them to Baṣrah.[24]

Ibn Aʿtham al- Kūfī uses this encounter between the two wives of the Prophet to highlight more sharply their rivalry and thus present a clearly Shīʿī view of the entire episode. Here Umm Salamah answers ʿĀ'ishah's invitation angrily: "Woe to you, O ʿĀ'ishah, would you rebel against ʿAlī the cousin of the Messenger of God, after both the Muhājirūn and the Anṣār willingly offered him *bayʿah*?" While Umm Salamah recounted ʿAlī's excellences, ʿAbd Allāh son of al-Zubayr stood listening at the door. He cried out, "We know well your animosity towards the family of al-Zubayr!" Umm Salamah retorted, "Do you think that the Immigrants and Supporters would accept your father al-Zubayr and his fellow Ṭalḥah while ʿAlī ibn Abī Ṭālib, who is the master (*walī*) of every man and woman of faith, lives?" ʿAbd Allāh denied having heard such a designation of ʿAlī from the Prophet. Umm Salamah insisted that his aunt, ʿĀ'ishah, had heard the Prophet say, "ʿAlī is my representative (*khalīfah*) over you, both during my life and after my death. Anyone who disobeys him disobeys me." She then asked ʿĀ'ishah, "Do you testify or not, O ʿĀ'ishah, that you heard this?" "Yes, by God I did," she replied.[25]

24. al-Yaʿqūbī, vol. 2, p. 180–181.
25. al-Kūfī, vol. 2, pp. 160–161.

Umm Salamah's testimony concerning 'Alī's right to the caliphal office, corroborated by 'Ā'ishah herself, as well as numerous other attestations of his unique relationship to the Prophet, lead us to think that 'Alī may have considered his caliphate to be a return to the Prophetic model of Madīnah. He appears to have consciously preferred uprightness and strict veracity over compromise and diplomacy. Strict veracity and uprightness were of course necessary virtues in the formation of the first Islamic commonwealth, yet the Prophet had always balanced these virtues with prudent diplomacy and compromise. 'Alī seems to have sought to emulate the Prophet's normative conduct, but he lacked the Prophet's far-sighted political flexibility, and that, in the end, brought about his downfall.

Both 'Alī's cousin Ibn 'Abbās and his eldest son al-Ḥasan discerned the dangers inherent in his uncompromising idealism and counselled political realism, but to no avail. Ibn 'Abbās advised 'Alī to grant Ṭalḥah and al-Zubayr lucrative posts, simply to assuage their love of power and material wealth. However, 'Alī revoked their appointments precisely because of this attachment. Ḥasan is also reported to have confronted 'Alī, as he was on his way to Baṣrah to face the rebellious Ṭalḥah and al-Zubayr, with what he considered to be grave errors of judgment on the part of his father.

Ḥasan reminded his father that he had advised him to leave Madīnah when 'Uthmān was besieged, so that he would not witness 'Uthmān's death, but 'Alī had refused. And, when 'Uthmān was killed, he had advised him not to accept the allegiance of the people of Madīnah until he received the delegations of all other regions with their *bay'ah*, and again 'Alī had not heeded his counsel. Ḥasan now advised his father to sit quietly in his house and wait until the sedition stirred by 'Ā'ishah and her two accomplices was resolved. Once again, 'Alī ignored his son's counsel, this time on the ground that he could not turn back and retain his credibility as the imām of the community. He maintained, regarding Ḥasan's other pieces of advice, that when 'Uthmān was besieged, he too was besieged. He also argued that it was not necessary to wait for the *bay'ah* of the people of other regions when he already had the consensus of the people of Madīnah. As for the rebellion of Ṭalḥah and al-Zubayr, "That is," 'Alī asserted, "a disgrace for the people of Islam." Nor could he now sit at home, "For," he said, "if I do not look into my own obligations in this affair, then who will?" Since, moreover, the people had freely offered him their allegiance, 'Alī concluded, "I will fight those who oppose me with those who follow me until God judges between them and me, and He is the best of judges."[26]

The battle was fought, Muslims on both sides were killed, and 'Alī's forces were victorious. Because the battle was fought at all, the whole of the Muslim *ummah* lost. In theory, Islam is a community religion based on the principle of the brotherhood of faith of all Muslims.[27] Furthermore, this communitarian characteristic of the faith is supposed to transcend all sectarian, social, and political differences. The Battle of the Camel was a flagrant violation of that fundamental Islamic tenet. Not only did it violate the principle of Muslim unity, it also sanctioned the use of force and even bloodshed as a means of achieving political ends.

This battle, moreover, precipitated a moral and religious crisis for pious Muslims. It put into serious question the integrity, and hence leadership, of some of the Prophet's closest and most venerated Companions. It raised anew the old issue of religious verses tribal loyalty, which had bedevilled the caliphal office from its inception. It stirred, as well, the old blood feuds which had devastated pre-Islamic Arab society, and which Islam was meant to eradicate.[28]

The dilemma, which the prospect of such armed conflicts created for the generality of Muslims, was succinctly expressed by Ṭāriq b. Shihāb, a devotee of 'Alī, who met the latter on his way to Baṣrah. Ṭāriq wondered, "Should we fight against the Mother of the Faithful ['Ā'ishah] and the disciple (*ḥawārī*) of the Messenger of God

26. al-Ṭabarī, vol. 4, pp. 456–458. See also Ibn Abī al-Ḥadīd, vol. 1, pp. 226–227.
27. See Q.3:103 and 49:10.
28. The Qur'ān sharply condemns such feuds and calls on Muslims to "hold fast to the rope of God altogether" as brothers in the faith (3:103).

[al-Zubayr]? This is indeed a grave matter." But, he further mused, "Should I then abandon 'Alī who is the first man to have accepted faith in God, and who is the cousin of the Messenger of God and his vicegerent? This is an even graver matter!"[29]

Perhaps the most serious consequence of the Battle of the Camel was that 'Alī lost moral and political authority as leader, or imām of the Muslims. Thus a number of his new governors were forcibly prevented from assuming their offices. And when 'Alī wrote to Mu'āwiyah, demanding his oath of allegiance, the latter sent in reply a sheet of paper – blank except for the opening invocation: "In the name of God, the All-merciful, the Compassionate." Mu'āwiyah added threat to insult by instructing his emissary to tell 'Alī that he had left sixty thousand elders in Damascus mourning the death of 'Uthmān under his bloodstained shirt, which was displayed for them upon the pulpit of the city's central mosque. "These men," he continued, "will accept nothing but revenge." 'Alī asked, "From whom?" "From the thread of your own life," the man answered. 'Alī strenuously denied any involvement in 'Uthmān's murder, exclaiming, "O God, I declare my innocence, before You, of the blood of 'Uthmān."[30]

Mu'āwiyah's Opposition

The conflict between 'Alī and Mu'āwiyah rested on 'Alī's conviction of the unquestionable legitimacy of his caliphal authority and on Mu'āwiyah's increasing insistence on his own right to be heir (*walī*) to 'Uthmān in demanding retaliation for his blood. This claim, moreover, became the basis of Mu'āwiyah's bid for the caliphate. Ibn Qutaybah reports that Mu'āwiyah received the allegiance of the people of Syria as 'Uthmān's successor soon after 'Alī had assumed the caliphal office.[31]

The points of contention are clearly set forth in a long letter written by 'Alī to Mu'āwiyah, as reported by Naṣr b. Muzāḥim (d. 213/828) one of the earliest historians of the civil war of Ṣiffīn. 'Alī argued:

29. Ibn Abī al-Ḥadīd, vol. 1, p. 226; see also al-Ṭabarī, vol. 4, p. 455.
30. al-Ṭabarī, vol. 4, p. 445.
31. Ibn Qutaybah, vol. 1, p. 99.

> My *bay'ah* from the people of Madīnah is binding upon you even though you are in Syria. This is because they are the people who gave the same oath of allegiance to Abū Bakr, 'Umar and 'Uthmān. Thus, others who were present had no choice in the matter, and those who were far away have no right to object, for the prerogative of consultation (*shūrā*) belongs only to the Muhājirūn and Anṣār. Once they have agreed on a man as the imām and declared him by name, their decision must be accepted. If, moreover, anyone deviates from their decision either by denouncing it or coveting [the caliphate for himself], they must bring him back. If he resists, they must fight him, for he will not have followed the way of the people of faith.

'Alī then recounted the fate that had befallen Ṭalḥah and al-Zubayr after they revoked their *bay'ah*. Turning next to the question of avenging 'Uthmān, 'Alī counseled Mu'āwiyah to join the Muslims in their pledge of fealty and promised to judge the murderers in accordance with the Book of God. "As for your desire for the caliphate," 'Alī continued, "it is like the deception of an infant away from its mother's milk. For, if you were to view this matter with your reason rather than your vain desire, you would find me the most innocent man of the Quraysh of the blood of 'Uthmān." 'Alī concluded with the reminder that Mu'āwiyah had been among those pardoned by the Prophet on the day of the conquest of Makkah and thus had no legitimate claim to the caliphate.[32]

It was observed above that a primary cause for the insurrection of Ṭalḥah and al-Zubayr was their desire for wealth and prestige. We also saw that 'Alī was uncompromising in his refusal to grant favors, either to buy loyalty or to mollify opposition. This clash between religious fundamentals and political or social expediency is graphically portrayed in two anecdotes. The first is a brief exchange between 'Alī and his nephew 'Abd Allāh b. Ja'far b. Abī Ṭālib. 'Abd Allāh asked for financial help from the central treasury, for he was forced to sell the fodder of his animals to feed his children. 'Alī replied, "No by God, I

32. Abū al-Faḍl Naṣr b. Muzāḥim b. Sayyār al-Minqarī, *Waq'at Ṣiffīn*, ed. 'Abd al-Salām Muḥammad Hārūn (Beirut: Dār al-Jīl, n.d.), pp. 29–30.

have nothing for you, unless you command your uncle to steal and give to you."[33]

The second is 'Alī's reply to the advice of some of his followers that he favor the notables of the Arabs, particularly the Quraysh, over non-Arab clients (*mawālī*) in the allotment of stipends, as did Mu'āwiyah. In this way, they argued, 'Alī would secure the loyalty of the Arabs and strengthen his own authority. 'Alī answered, "Do you wish me to seek victory through oppression? By God, I will never do that so long as the sun rises and stars appear in the sky. For, by God, if this wealth belonged to me, I would distribute it equally among them. How much more imperative is this when these revenues are theirs by right!"[34]

'Alī's strict egalitarian justice with regard to the distribution of wealth caused, not only Ṭalḥah and al-Zubayr, but also many of the elders of the Quraysh – including some of his close relatives and strong supporters – to turn against him. Perhaps sensitive to this disaffection, and in anticipation of a direct confrontation with Mu'āwiyah, 'Alī is reported to have written to his governors calling on them for support.

He wrote and admonished al-Ash'ath b. Qays, one of those among 'Uthmān's governors whom he had confirmed in their posts, saying, "Your administrative post is not a private source of wealth for you to devour, but a trust. You have in your hands some of God's wealth, and you are one of its treasurers until you surrender it to me. I will not be the worst of your masters if you act uprightly."[35] Al-Ash'ath, a pragmatic old man, was generally lukewarm in his loyalty to 'Alī. He was troubled by 'Alī's letter because he feared that 'Alī would bring him to account for the large sums of the revenues of Adharbījān that he had misappropriated during his tenure as 'Uthmān's governor of the province. He thus contemplated going over to Mu'āwiyah, but his

33. Abū Isḥaq Ibrahīm b. Muḥammad b. Sa'īd b. Hilāl al-Thaqafī, *Kitāb al-ghārāt aw al-istinfār wal-ghārāt*, ed. 'Abd al-Zahrā' al-Ḥusaynī al-Khaṭīb (Beirut: Dār al-Aḍwā', 1407/1987), p. 43.
34. Ibid., p. 48.
35. Ibn Muzāḥim, p. 20.

close associates rebuked him and compelled him to remain loyal to ʿAlī .[36]

ʿAlī was not as well served by his own brother ʿAqīl b. Abī Ṭālib, who went to him in Kūfah requesting financial help for the support of his large family. ʿAlī offered to give him his own stipend when he received it, but ʿAqīl insisted on large sums from the central treasury. ʿAlī asked his brother to stay with him until the following Friday; after the prayers he asked, "What would you say about a man who betrays the trust of all these people?" "Evil indeed is such a man," ʿAqīl replied. ʿAlī retorted, "But you are asking me to defraud them all by granting you illicit wealth!"

ʿAqīl angrily left his brother and went to Muʿāwiyah. On the day of his arrival, Muʿāwiyah made him a generous gift of a hundred and seventy thousand dirhams. He then asked, "O Abū Yazīd [ʿAqīl's agnomen], who is better for you, I or ʿAlī?" ʿAqīl answered, "I found ʿAlī more concerned with his soul than with me, but I find you more concerned with me than with your own soul."[37]

To many, ʿAlī's strict adherence to the religious precept of equality was a great strength. To others, as we have seen, it was not only foolishness but betrayal. Muʿāwiyah played on these tensions to his own political advantage. No doubt aware of ʿAlī's high status in the Muslim community, as well as the legitimacy of ʿAlī's *bayʿah*, he was likewise aware of the weakness of his own claim to be the legal requiter of ʿUthmān's blood in the place of the latter's own legitimate heirs. At first he moved cautiously in voicing this claim and consequently in challenging ʿAlī's caliphal authority. Emboldened by the Battle of the Camel – its causes and consequences – and by the continuing erosion of ʿAlī's support, Muʿāwiyah became more insistent.

Muʿāwiyah was further encouraged by the unquestioning obedience of his Syrian army as well as the support and loyalty of the people

36. See al-Kūfī, vol. 2, p. 371.
37. Ibn Abī al-Ḥadīd, vol. 4, p. 92. Ibn Abī al-Ḥadīd includes ʿAqīl in a long list of Companions and Successors who deserted or opposed ʿAlī because he did not favor them with special monetary gifts. See vol. 4, pp. 74 ff.

of Syria. In contrast, 'Alī's fighters were largely semi-nomadic independent-minded men unused to the unquestioned authority of a single chief or ruler. The sharp contrast between the urbane people of Syria and the largely tribal people of Iraq was dramatically expressed by a man called al-Ḥajjāj b. Khuzaymah,[38] who went to Mu'āwiyah with the news of 'Uthmān's death, accusing the men of the house of Hāshim of being responsible for it. Al-Ḥajjāj is reported to have been the first man to address Mu'āwiyah as *amir al-mu'minīn* (Commander of the Faithful). He said:

> I tell you, O Commander of the Faithful, that you have a source of power against 'Alī that he does not have against you. You have people who say nothing when you speak, nor ask "Why?" when you command. But there are with 'Alī people who speak when he speaks and question him when he commands. Therefore, the few who are with you are better than the many who are with him.

Al-Ḥajjāj went on to argue that, while 'Alī would not accept to give up Syria for Iraq, Mu'āwiyah would be happy with Syria alone.[39]

In spite of the deep hostility between 'Alī and Mu'āwiyah, both appear to have preferred to resolve their quarrels through mediation and diplomacy rather than bloodshed. Thus a number of emissaries and letters were exchanged in an effort to defuse the situation. Jarīr b. 'Abd Allāh al-Bajli, a notable of the Yamanite Arabs and 'Alī's governor over the district of Hamadhān, was 'Alī's first emissary to Mu'āwiyah. His mission was to convince Mu'āwiyah and his Syrian supporters – many of whom were fellow Yamanites – to give *bay'ah* to 'Alī and yield to his judgment regarding the murder of 'Uthmān and its perpetrators.

Jarīr called on the Syrians and their governor to pledge allegiance to 'Alī, arguing that "this religion cannot tolerate sedition and the Arabs cannot withstand the sword." As for 'Uthmān's death, Jarīr added, "it has defied those who witnessed it, let alone those who were

38. According to Ibn Muzāḥim (p. 79), he was al-Ḥajjāj b. al-Ṣimmah.
39. Ibid.; see also, Ibn Qutaybah, vol. 1, p. 76.

not even present. Moreover, people gave *bay'ah* to 'Alī without regard to anyone being victimized or seeking vengeance."[40] But Jarīr's arguments and entreaties were to no avail.

Mu'āwiyah rested his right to the governorship of Syria on the grounds that he had been appointed by 'Umar and confirmed by 'Uthmān and, hence, 'Alī had no authority over him. Jarīr rejected this reasoning and countered that such a practice, if allowed, would make it impossible for a ruler to revoke any of the decisions of his predecessors, and would deprive him of any real power. It would, moreover, inevitably lead to chaos and illicit authority. Mu'āwiyah gave Jarīr no answer, asking for more time to think things over.

As Jarīr waited, Mu'āwiyah quietly sought to consolidate his own power. To this end, he gathered the notables of his Syrian subjects to ascertain their loyalty and to see where they stood on the issue of 'Uthmān's death and on his own right to demand requital for 'Uthmān's blood. He addressed them saying:

> Praise be to God who made the firm supports of Islam its pillars (*arkān*) and made the sacred laws the proofs of faith; a faith whose torch shall forever burn in the holy land, which He made the abode of His prophets and righteous servants. God then made the people of Syria to dwell in this land, accepting it for them and them for it. For, He knew from eternity their obedience and sincere counsel to His representatives (*khulafā'*) who abide by His commands and protect His religion and inviolable sanctions.

Mu'āwiyah then reminded the assembled men that he was the deputy (*khalīfah*) of both 'Umar and 'Uthmān over them, that he was 'Uthmān's heir, and that 'Uthmān had been unjustly killed. He then demanded, "I wish to know what you really hold in your hearts concerning the murder of 'Uthmān." They all pledged allegiance to him on condition that he exact revenge for 'Uthmān's blood.[41]

The ramifications of this important oration go well beyond its immediate purpose, which was to consolidate Mu'āwiyah's authority in

40. Ibn Muzāḥim, p. 30.
41. Ibid., pp. 31–32; see also al-Kūfī, vol. 2, pp. 380–381.

Syria. Its far-reaching significance lies in the fact that it marks the beginning of a conscious effort on the part of later Umayyad rulers to establish, in the holy land of Syria, alternative sites for pious pilgrimages to Makkah and Madīnah. The aim of this endeavor was twofold: to enhance the significance of Syria, and consequently of Damascus as the new capital of the caliphate; and, to turn people away from Arabia, where Umayyad rule was generally unpopular. The success of this strategy may be judged by the fact that pilgrimage to *bayt al-maqdis*, the "Holy House" of Jerusalem, has become an integral part of the *ḥajj* pilgrimage.

Mu'āwiyah further strengthened his chances of success in his bid for power by enticing 'Amr b. al-'Āṣ to be his close collaborator in the fight against 'Alī. 'Amr was a respected Qurayshite Companion, a noted military strategist, and an astute politician. The account of 'Amr's acceptance of Mu'āwiyah's invitation may be largely apocryphal. It is, nonetheless, highly instructive, in that it graphically depicts the popular perception of the nature of the conflict between 'Alī and Mu'āwiyah as well as the place of the two men in the Islamic moral and political value-system.

Unable to make up his mind, 'Amr is reported to have asked his two sons for advice. 'Abd Allāh, a pious Companion and respected traditionist, said:

> I see that the Prophet of God died and was still pleased with you, as were the two caliphs [Abū Bakr and 'Umar] after him. Furthermore, 'Uthmān was killed while you were away from him. Therefore stay in your house, for you will never be chosen for the caliphate. Nor should you yourself choose to be one of Mu'āwiyah's retinue for a meagre portion of this world, which may become the cause of your wretchedness and perdition.

Muḥammad, 'Amr's younger and worldly minded son, advised his father to join the people of Syria in demanding vengeance for the blood of 'Uthmān, so that he might be "a head rather than a tail" in any effort to resolve the matter. 'Amr observed, "As for you, 'Abd Allāh, you have advised me to do that which is best for me in the hereafter. But you, Muḥammad, you advised me to do that which is best for me in this world."[42] Still unable to make up his mind, 'Amr first ordered Wardān, a pious and perceptive servant of his, to set out and then to "stop and unload." Perceiving his master's perplexity, Wardān commented:

> This world and the world to come are fighting over your heart and you stand confused between the two. You say that with 'Alī is the hereafter but not this world, yet the hereafter has much to compensate for the loss of the goods of this world. With Mu'āwiyah, on the other hand, is this world, but this world is no substitute for the world to come.

Wardān then advised his master not to go. "For," he said, "if the people of religion prevail, you would live in the clemency of their faith. But if the people of this world prevail, they will surely seek your advice."[43]

'Amr no doubt saw his venture with Mu'āwiyah purely as an opportunity to regain authority over Egypt and its fabulous wealth, having himself conquered the territory during 'Umar's caliphate. Perhaps wishing to ascertain 'Amr's negotiating strategy, Mu'āwiyah said, "O Abū 'Abd Allāh, I call you to the *jihād* against this man who disobeyed his Lord, killed the Caliph, sowed discord, brought disunity into the community and severed the connection with his next-of-kin." "*Jihād* against whom?" 'Amr asked. "Against 'Alī," Mu'āwiyah answered. But 'Amr declared, "You and 'Alī are by no means equal in honor and prestige. You have neither his migration [*hijrah*], his priority [in Islam], his Companionship [with the Prophet], his *jihād*, nor his religious learning and knowledge." 'Amr then asked, "What would you give me if I collaborate with you in your fight against him?" "I shall give you Egypt, as a tasty morsel for you to devour," Mu'āwiyah answered.[44]

Ibn Abī al-Ḥadīd reports that it was 'Amr who advised Mu'āwiyah to spread the rumor that 'Alī had killed 'Uthmān. The people of Syria came to be so convinced of the truth of this rumor that, when 'Alī again

42. Ibn Muzāḥim, p. 34. al-Ya'qūbī sees a direct link between Jarīr's visit, which disturbed Mu'āwiyah, and the latter's invitation to 'Amr to be his confident; see al-Ya'qūbī, vol. 2, p. 184.
43. Ibn Abī al-Ḥadīd, vol. 2, p. 63.
44. Ibn Muzāḥim, pp. 37–38.

wrote to Mu'āwiyah calling upon him to offer his pledge of allegiance, they threatened, "By God, if you give allegiance to 'Alī we will drive you out of our Syria or kill you." Mu'āwiyah reassured them, "I would never oppose you. I am only a man of the people of Syria."[45]

It was important for both 'Alī and Mu'āwiyah to have on their side men of the Immigrants and Supporters, Qur'ān reciters, and other men known for their piety and learning. 'Alī's army included many such men who fought and died for him. Mu'āwiyah wrote to the people of Madīnah for their support against 'Alī in demanding requital for 'Uthmān's blood. 'Alī must be accountable for the crime, Mu'āwiyah argued, because he gave shelter to 'Uthmān's murderers. Thus, Mu'āwiyah suggested that 'Alī turn 'Uthmān's murderers over to him and the people of Syria for punishment, and that a new caliph be chosen through general consultation among the Muslims. He himself, Mu'āwiyah asserted, was not interested in the caliphate. The people of Madīnah rejected his request, accusing him and 'Amr b. al-'Āṣ of deception and treachery.[46]

Unperturbed by the harsh reply of the people of Madīnah, Mu'āwiyah wrote to 'Abd Allāh b. 'Umar b. al-Khaṭṭāb, Sa'd b. Abī Waqqāṣ, and Muḥammad b. Maslamah to enlist their support. He suggested to 'Abd Allāh b. 'Umar that he join those championing the cause of 'Uthmān and himself assume the caliphate, or, a new caliph could be chosen through general consultation. 'Abd Allāh answered that Mu'āwiyah was deluded in thinking that he would follow him after having deserted 'Alī, Ṭalḥah and al-Zubayr, as well as 'Ā'ishah, the Mother of the Faithful. He continued:

> I received no instructions or pact from the Messenger of God concerning this affair. For this reason I chose caution and neutrality concerning it. I said to myself that if this affair is one of right guidance, then it is a good which I have missed, but if it is an error, then it is an evil from which I have been delivered.[47]

45. Ibn Abī al-Ḥadīd, vol. 2, p. 72.
46. al-Kūfī, vol. 2, pp. 414–417.
47. Ibn Muzāḥim, pp. 72–73.

With regard to the second man Mu'āwiyah approached, it should be recalled that Sa'd b. Abī Waqqāṣ was one of the six men of 'Umar's consultative council. Mu'āwiyah therefore based his reasoning, in the letter he wrote to him, on this important fact. He argued:

> The most worthy among the people of upholding 'Uthmān's cause are the people of consultation of the Quraysh, who confirmed his right and chose him over others. Furthermore, both Ṭalḥah and al-Zubayr rose up in support of his cause, and they are your associates in this affair and your peers in Islam. Likewise, the Mother of the Faithful ['A¯'ishah] rose up. Therefore, do not disdain what they preferred or reject what they favored.

Here too, Mu'āwiyah advised that 'Alī's caliphate be revoked and a new caliph be chosen through general consultation. Like 'Abd Allāh b. 'Umar, Sa'd rejected Mu'āwiyah's invitation and vowed neutrality:

> 'Umar included in the *shūrā* council only the men of the Quraysh who were lawfully qualified for the caliphate. No one among us was more qualified for it than any other except through our general consensus in choosing him. 'Alī, however, possessed all the qualities we possessed, but we did not possess all his qualities. Moreover, this is an affair whose beginning we hated as we did its end. As for Ṭalḥah and al-Zubayr, it would have been better for them to have stayed in their homes; and may God forgive the Mother of the Faithful for what she did.[48]

The third man Mu'āwiyah approached, Muḥammad b. Maslamah, was a man of the Anṣār, not of the Quraysh. The Anṣār, as we have already seen, were known for their loyalty to 'Alī and their antipathy towards the men of the Quraysh, and the sons of Umayyah in particular. Thus Mu'āwiyah's letter to him was harsh and reproachful. Muḥammad's neutral position towards the murder of 'Uthmān and the civil strife it engendered was based on an alleged Prophetic *ḥadīth* tradition which forbade "people of the prayers (*ṣalāt*) [that is the Muslims]" to fight one another.

Mu'āwiyah first argued that Muḥammad should have deplored for

48. Ibid., pp. 74–75; see also al-Ya'qūbī, vol. 2, pp. 184–187.

the Muslims what the Prophet had deplored for them. He then asked, "Did you not see what befell 'Uthmān at the hands of the people of the prayers on the day of the house?"[49] "As for your people," Mu'āwiyah continued, "they disobeyed God and abandoned 'Uthmān, and God will question both them and you concerning this matter on the Day of Resurrection." Muḥammad answered:

> There were men of the Quraysh who took a neutral position in this affair even without having received from the Messenger of God what I received concerning it, for he informed me of what was to happen long before it did. When, therefore, I witnessed the fulfilment of what he had foretold, I broke my sword and decided to remain in my house. This is because I found in the affair neither good (*ma'rūf*) to enjoin, nor evil (*munkar*) to dissuade therefrom. As for you, O Mu'āwiyah, you seek nothing but this world and follow nothing but your own capricious desires. For, even though you support 'Uthmān after his death, you abandoned him during his life.[50]

The situation between 'Ali and Mu'āwiyah was causing a rupture in the Muslim community, a rupture that soon found expression in the civil war known as the Battle of Ṣiffīn. Before we turn to a brief examination of some aspects of the Ṣiffīn conflict and its aftermath, it may be useful in light of our discussion so far to enquire once more into Mu'āwiyah's real motive in opposing 'Alī. This question has been the subject of much debate among Muslim historians and traditionists as well as Western scholars. It has been argued that, had 'Alī confirmed him in his post and given him a free hand to rule Syria as he had done under both 'Umar and 'Uthmān, Mu'āwiyah would not have risen against a ruling caliph, however much he may have deplored 'Uthmān's tragic death. This was, as we have seen, the view of both al-Mughīrah b. Shu'bah and Ibn 'Abbās.

Two closely interrelated questions demand attention in this regard. The first is whether and when Mu'āwiyah began to covet the caliphate.

49. 'Uthmān's long siege in his house and his subsequent assassination are known as *yawm al-dār* (day of the house).
50. al-Kūfī, vol. 2, p. 424.

The second is whether he advanced his sole right to demand retaliation for 'Uthmān's blood simply as a pretext for achieving this goal, or if he was truly sincere in demanding retaliation for the blood of a near relative. As for the second question, Mu'āwiyah was, as we have seen, repeatedly accused of having betrayed 'Uthmān by failing to come to his rescue during the fateful siege. With regard to the first and more important question, Mu'āwiyah may have contemplated the possibility of his accession to the caliphate, or at least of gaining absolute authority over Syria, following the Battle of the Camel during which he simply adopted a wait and see attitude.

As events unfolded, however, Mu'āwiyah appears to have considered the possibilities of at least two scenarios arising from his active opposition to 'Alī. The first was expressed in his suggestion to Jarīr, 'Alī's envoy, that 'Alī cede for him Syria and Egypt and keep for himself Iraq and the Ḥijāz. Mu'āwiyah may have hoped that he would then, in the event of 'Alī's death or removal from office, be a natural choice for the caliphate. This is suggested by his insistence that he be free from any obligation of allegiance to anyone, including 'Alī.[51] As we shall see, Mu'āwiyah made the same proposal in his indirect negotiations with 'Alī for ending the conflict of Ṣiffīn. The second scenario involved a prolonged struggle with a view to revoking 'Alī's caliphate and Mu'āwiyah himself assuming authority.

The clearest assertion of Mu'āwiyah's claim to the caliphate was made to the people of Syria shortly before the Battle of Ṣiffīn. Mu'āwiyah argued:

> Tell me, why is 'Alī son of Abū Ṭālib more worthy of this office than me? By God, I was the amanuensis of the Messenger of God. My sister [Umm Ḥabībah, daughter of Abū Sufyān] was wife to the Messenger of God. I was, moreover, governor for both 'Umar b. al-Khaṭṭāb and 'Uthmān b. 'Affān. My mother was Hind daughter of 'Utbah b. Rabī'ah [meaning that she too was of noble lineage], and my father was Abū Sufyān b. Ḥarb. Furthermore, although the people of the Ḥijāz and Iraq swore allegiance to 'Alī, the people of Syria pledged allegiance to me. The people of all

51. See Ibn Muzāḥim, p. 52.

> three regions are equal [in prestige], and whoever can seize a thing by force, it shall be his.[52]

The last point of this argument, namely the legitimacy of political power gained by force rather than consultation or moral suasion, became a precedent that most Muslim rulers, in one way or another, followed thenceforth. This unfortunate practice was even sanctioned by classical political legal theorists.[53]

A similar argument, but with an even more defiant tone, was made in a letter said to have been addressed by Mu'āwiyah to 'Alī shortly before the latter crossed the Euphrates river to meet him and his army on the plane of Ṣiffīn. Mu'āwiyah began by arguing that, had 'Alī followed the example of his three predecessors, he would not have rebelled against him. He added that another reason for his rebellion was 'Alī's betrayal of 'Uthmān. Mu'āwiyah continued: "The people of the Ḥijāz were judges over the rest of the Muslims only when they had the truth on their side. But when they abandoned it, the people of Syria became judges over the people of the Ḥijāz as well as the peoples of all other regions." Mu'āwiyah further asserted that, while 'Alī may have had an argument against Ṭalḥah and al-Zubayr because they gave their *bay'ah* to him and then revoked it, he had not given his *bay'ah*. He similarly argued that 'Alī had no claim of loyalty over the people of Syria because they never pledged allegiance to him as had the people of Baṣrah. Mu'āwiyah presented his conflict with 'Alī as a quarrel between two men of equal status. His conclusion, "As for your priority in Islam, your close kinship with the Messenger and your status in the house of Hāshim, I shall not dispute them,"[54] implies socio-political equality between the Umayyad and Hashimite houses of Quraysh.

Whatever Mu'āwiyah's motives may have been, it seems that he did

52. al-Kūfī, vol. 2, p. 428–429.
53. For a discussion of medieval Islamic political theorists, see Erwin Rosenthal, *Political Thought in Medieval Islam* (Cambridge: Cambridge University Press, 1958), esp. pp. 21–109.
54. For this letter, see al-Kūfī, vol. 2, pp. 429–430.

not anticipate the radical results of his opposition to ʿAlī. Judging by his subsequent long and relatively peaceful rule, which was based on his diplomatic abilities rather than on direct confrontation with his opponents, it seems plausible that he would have preferred a protracted period of unarmed opposition to open warfare. Whether or not the Battle of Ṣiffīn, the result of his opposition to ʿAlī, was consciously instigated by either or Muʿāwiyah or ʿAlī must remain an open question.

The Battle of Ṣiffīn

The Battle of the Camel was a serious but brief encounter largely between ʿAlī's Kufan supporters and his Baṣran opponents. The Battle of Ṣiffīn, in contrast, involved the populations of Syria and Iraq and was a protracted and bloody conflict which dragged on for weeks.[55] Furthermore, while the two conflicts arose from similar motives and circumstances, that of Ṣiffīn had more far reaching consequences and claimed many more lives. In fact, the Ṣiffīn civil war irreparably deepened the split of the Muslim community and altered the course of its history.

Even more blatantly than in the Battle of the Camel, a quest for power and wealth was the primary motive behind this first civil war in Islam. Muʿāwiyah, one of its chief protagonists, used wealth, power, and clever stratagems to great advantage. He was, as well, greatly helped by the disenchantment of many pious Muslims with both ʿAlī's heavy-handed and uncompromising policies and with his own rebellion against ʿAlī, a legitimately appointed and highly respected imām of the Muslims. In the end, dismayed by the behaviour of their leaders, many who had at first sided with ʿAlī as the rightful caliph either withdrew their support, vowed absolute neu-

55. The Ṣiffīn conflict began with an initial skirmish in the month of Dhū al-ḥijjah A.H. 36–Ṣafar A.H. 37 (June–July 657). It ended, however inconclusively, in Ramaḍān A.H. 37 / February 658. This is the view of al-Ṭabarī (vol. 4, p. 575, and vol. 5, pp. 5 ff.). Ibn Muzāḥim, the historian of Ṣiffīn, puts the beginning of Ṣiffīn a month earlier, in Shawwāl, perhaps to avoid having the actual fighting begin during a sacred month (p. 131).

trality, or even sided with Mu'āwiyah in calling for the punishment of 'Uthmān's murderers.

It is beyond the scope and purpose of this study to go into the details of the war of Ṣiffīn. We shall rather limit ourselves, as we did with the Battle of the Camel, to a brief examination of the main events, actions, and personalities surrounding it. We shall pay special attention to some of the declarations – letters, speeches, and statements – relating to this tragic conflict and its causes and aftermath. This is because, we believe, such declarations reflect the attitudes and motivations of the men involved, as well as the sentiments of later Muslims as reflected in our sources.

It was observed earlier that pious Muslims were generally divided over the issue of Muslims fighting Muslims, some siding with 'Alī, others with Mu'āwiyah and still others choosing to remain neutral. 'Alī's reason for fighting Mu'āwiyah was, as we have seen, his conviction that the latter's rebellion was against "God's authority," represented by a legitimately appointed caliph. Mu'āwiyah, on the other hand, could only invoke revenge for 'Uthmān's murder as his reason for contesting 'Alī's authority. He first accused 'Alī of not having defended 'Uthmān, then of sheltering his murderers and finally of direct responsibility for this grave offence. Each of the two parties attempted to rationalize its position and thus gain supporters.

Mu'āwiyah was able to convince Shurḥabīl b. al-Ṣamt b. Jabalah al-Kindī, a man highly respected for both his noble lineage and piety, that "'Alī killed 'Uthmān." After some hesitation, Shurḥabīl became a staunch supporter of Mu'āwiyah and an eloquent spokesman for his right to seek requital for 'Uthmān's blood. Shurḥabīl met with great success in rallying the Syrians for Mu'āwiyah against 'Alī. He addressed the people of Ḥumṣ saying:

> O people, 'Alī murdered 'Uthmān b. 'Affān! A group of men [that is Ṭalḥah and al-Zubayr and their followers] rose up to avenge his blood, but 'Alī defeated and killed them all. He now holds sway over all the land except Syria. Furthermore, he is advancing with his sword on his shoulder and will soon overcome you, unless God decrees otherwise. There is

> no one more capable of meeting him in battle than Mu'āwiyah. Rise up therefore and show your prowess!

All the people answered his call except the ascetics (*nussāk*) of the city, who answered, "Our houses shall be both our graves and our places of worship."[56]

'Alī's camp, as we have already noted, lacked the solidarity and cohesion that Mu'āwiyah was able to muster in his Syrian army. This may have been due, in part, to the fact that many of 'Alī's supporters, as well as those who remained neutral, were more religiously scrupulous. Thus the Kufan followers of Ibn Mas'ūd said to 'Alī and his two sons, Ḥasan and Ḥusayn, who went to Kūfah to incite the men of the city to join their camp, "We shall go out with you, but we shall set our camp apart, so as to see for ourselves both your conduct and the conduct of the people of Syria. If we see people on either side violating God's sanctions and showing transgression (*baghī*), we shall turn against them."[57] 'Alī answered, "Welcome to you and your wise decision! This indeed is right comprehension (*fiqh*) of the religion and true knowledge of the *sunnah* [of the Prophet]. Anyone who does not accept this would be a transgressor and a traitor." Others, while recognizing the legitimacy of 'Alī's authority and hence their obligation to obey him, still could not bring themselves to fight fellow Muslims. They thus chose to join an expedition which was sent to defend the borders of the Rayy district of Persia.[58]

Questions of religious probity and proper conduct were of no less concern to 'Alī. He is reported to have written to the leaders of his army, which he had dispatched ahead of himself to Ṣiffīn, enjoining them not to transgress against people in the towns and villages; they were not to disturb them except when in dire need of food, or to ask for a guide if they lost their way. Regarding the relationship between

56. Ibn Muzāḥim, p. 50; see also pp. 44–52.
57. This decision accords with the Qur'ānic dictum "If two factions of the Muslims fight, make peace between them. But if one of them transgresses against the other, then fight the transgressing one until it returns to God's command" (Q.49:9).
58. For this and the preceding exchange, see Ibn Muzāḥim, p. 115.

himself and his army, and between his army and the people, 'Alī set these issues in the more general framework of the exercise of authority by the caliph and the interdependent responsibilities of the caliph and his subjects:

> God has made you all equal before the truth, the black and the red of you [that is, everyone regardless of ethnicity and lineage]. He likewise made your relationship to the ruler (*walī*) like that of a father to a child or a child to the father . . . Your right over him is that he should act justly among you and refrain from usurping your legally gained booty (*fay'*). If he does that, then it is incumbent upon you to obey and support him in whatever is consonant with the truth, and to defend God's authority. For, you are God's defenders in the land. Be therefore God's helpers and supporters in His religion.

'Alī concluded with the Qur'ānic injunction "Do not spread corruption in the earth after it has been set right, for God loves not those who spread corruption."[59]

Ṭabarī reports that 'Alī placed this large army under the leadership of Mālik al-Ashtar, whom he bid:

> Beware that you not engage in any fighting unless they attack first, for you must first meet with them, admonish them and hear what they have to say. Nor should their hostility cause you to do battle with them before you have admonished and apologised to them time after time.[60]

Ṭabarī further reports that 'Alī also enjoined his fighters not to initiate hostilities, but rather to fight only in self-defense when attacked. "For," he said, "you are by God's grace in the right, and refraining from attacking your opponents is another argument for you against them." He continued:

> If you engage in battle with a people and defeat them, do not kill anyone who runs away. Do not attack a wounded man, or expose the nakedness of anyone. Do not mutilate a dead person. If, moreover, you make your way into the tents of the people, do not violate their privacy, or enter a

59. Ibn Muzāḥim, pp. 125–126. There is no Qur'ānic verse with this specific phrase, but see 7:56 and 85, and 28:77.

60. al-Ṭabarī, vol. 4, p. 567.

> home except by permission [of its owner]. Nor should you seize as booty anything of their wealth, except what you find in their military camp. Do not harm women, even if they disgrace your family honor and insult your leaders and upright men.[61]

It has been repeatedly argued in this study that with ʿAlī's caliphate we witness a growing tension between religious principles and political expediencies. ʿAlī's letter to his fighters as well as the statements just quoted are a clear expression of this tension, particularly when measured against the behavior of some of both ʿAlī's and Muʿāwiyah's chief supporters.

Ibn Muzāḥim reports that before leaving Iraq ʿAlī dismissed al-Ashʿath b. Qays, a Yamanite, as a leader of the fighters of the tribes of Rabīʿah and Kindah and appointed in his place Ḥassān b. Makhdūj, a Muḍarite Arab. This awakened old tribal rivalries between the tribes of Muḍar and Rabīʿah on the one hand, and those of Kindah and other Yamanite tribes on the other. Thus al-Ashtar al-Nakhʿī, ʿAdī al-Ṭāʾī, and others of ʿAlī's closest Yamanite supporters, having interpreted ʿAlī's action as favoring his fellow Muḍarites over them, took offence. Muʿāwiyah attempted to use this incident as an opportunity to stir al-Ashʿath against ʿAlī, but without success.[62] This tribal rivalry was ʿAlī's great bane and ultimately led to his demise.

Another problem that directly contributed to ʿAlī's loss of morale at Ṣiffīn, of the caliphate, and ultimately of his life, was the aggressive individualism of his supporters. This ancient and persistent Bedouin trait is clearly depicted in an anecdote reported by Ibn Qutaybah. The main purpose of the following account may have been to discredit Ibn al-Kawwāʾ, who was one of ʿAlī's most notorious followers.[63] It nevertheless illustrates very well the contrast between Muʿāwiyah's urbane Syrian subjects and the radically individualistic and unruly tribesmen of ʿAlī's camp.

61. Ibid., vol. 5, p. 5; see also Ibn Muzāḥim, pp. 203–204.
62. Ibn Muzāḥim, pp. 138–139.
63. ʿAbd Allāh Ibn al-Kawwāʾ was the prayer leader of the *khawārij*, those who rebelled against ʿAlī. See below and *E.I.*^{2} s.v. "Ḥarūriyyah."

Prior to the conflict of Ṣiffīn, 'Alī ordered that state provisions (*al-mīrah*) for Syria be cut off. He sent Zaḥr b. Qays with a detachment to enforce his command. Zaḥr encountered a similar detachment sent by Mu'āwiyah under the leadership of his famous general al-Ḍaḥḥāk b. Qays, which Zaḥr easily defeated. Deeply disturbed by the news, Mu'āwiyah said to his followers, "I have received from one of the outlying districts news that is exceedingly grave." The men answered, "O Commander of the Faithful, we have nothing to do with what you received. We only hear and obey."

Hearing of this expression of unquestioning loyalty to Mu'āwiyah by his Syrian soldiers, 'Alī wished to test the loyalty of his own Iraqi fighters. He repeated Mu'āwiyah's words to them, whereupon Ibn al-Kawwā' and his fellows responded, "We have an opinion concerning every matter. Tell us, therefore, the news you have received, so that we may advise you." 'Alī wept, saying, "Fortunate indeed is the son of Hind with the concord of his followers in their loyalty to him and your discord in your loyalty to me. By God, his falsehood shall overcome your truth."[64]

This radical individualism, which often expressed itself in spontaneous and hasty emotional actions, was an important component of the clash of narrow tribal politics with religious morality in early Islam. The clash is further illustrated by an event that occurred at the banks of the Euphrates prior to the encounter of the two armies at Ṣiffīn. Mu'āwiyah's soldiers preceded 'Alī and his fighters to the water and vowed to block their way to it at all cost. Their determination was expressed by al-Walīd b. 'Uqbah who vowed: "I shall deny them water as they did deny it 'Uthmān b. 'Affān. They besieged him for forty days and denied him the taste of cool water and good food. I shall kill them with thirst, may God kill them."[65]

Ya'qūbī's report of this event demonstrates more sharply the point under discussion. Mu'āwiyah's own men pleaded with him not to let

64. Ibn Qutaybah, vol. 1, p. 127.
65. Ibid., vol. 1, pp. 161–162.

the people die of thirst, for, there were "among them the [innocent] slave, handmaid, and hired-hand." But he insisted, "May God not allow me and Abū Sufyān to drink from the Spring (*ḥawḍ*) of the Messenger of God[66] if they ever drink of this water." When, however, 'Alī's fighters quickly drove them away from the river bank, Mu'āwiyah's men were greatly alarmed. 'Amr b. al-'Āṣ, who strongly objected to the unseemly behavior of blocking even an enemy from water, reassured Mu'āwiyah saying, "'Alī would not deem it lawful to do to you and your men what you and your men have done to them."[67] The contrast is clear: While Mu'āwiyah uses religious language to effect a military and political stratagem, in al-'Āṣ's statement is contained the recognition, shared by both 'Alī's supporters and detractors, of 'Alī's commitment to religious imperatives over military or political expediency.

Following this minor incident, 'Alī and Mu'āwiyah observed a truce for the sacred month of Muḥarram, as fighting was prohibited during the sacred months. Emissaries followed one another from both sides in hope that actual fighting could be averted. The points at issue in these meetings, and that seem to lie behind the entire conflict of Ṣiffīn, were both religious and political in nature. A summary of the exchanges of two such meetings will suffice to illustrate some of the differing perceptions involved.

In our first example, a group of men headed by Ḥabīb b. Maslamah[68] came from Mu'āwiyah's camp to 'Alī. Ḥabīb argued:

> 'Uthmān b. 'Affān was a rightly guided (*mahdī*) caliph who abided by the Book of God and always strove to fulfil God's commands. Yet you ['Alī and

66. *Ḥawḍ al-kawthar* is a paradisal spring that God will give to the Prophet on the day of Resurrection to give its sweet waters to those who loved him and the people of his house in this world, and to turn their opponents away thirsty. See M. Ayoub, *Redemptive Suffering in Islam: A Study of the Devotional Aspects of 'A¯shūrā' in Twelver Shi'ism* (The Hague: Mouton Publishers, 1978), pp. 205–209.
67. al-Ya'qūbī, vol. 2, pp. 187–188.
68. Ḥabīb was a notable of the Quraysh who was born about twelve years before the Prophet's death and died in A.H. 42 Hence, his Companionship (*ṣuḥbah*) of the Prophet has been questioned. See Ibn Ḥajar, vol. 1, p. 309.

> his followers] found his life to be a burden to you and his death too long in coming. Thus you rushed at him and killed him. Turn [you, ʻAlī] over to us ʻUthmān's murderers therefore, so that we may kill them in retaliation for his blood. If, however, you say that you did not kill him, then relinquish your authority over the people, so that they may choose by common consensus the man who will rule over them.[69]

ʻAlī began his rebuttal, not by addressing the issue of ʻUthmān's death, but by affirming the legitimacy of his own authority. He argued that although Abū Bakr and ʻUmar had wrongfully assumed the caliphate, which by right belonged to the immediate family (*ahl al-bayt*) of the Prophet, still, "they lived upright lives and dealt justly with the *ummah*." As for ʻUthmān: "The people found fault with some of his actions," ʻAlī continued, "and thus attacked and killed him." After censuring the rebellion of Ṭalḥah and al-Zubayr, who had wrongfully revoked their *bayʻah* to him, ʻAlī said to Muʻāwiyah's emissaries, "I now call you to the Book of God and the *sunnah* of your Prophet. I enjoin you to uproot falsehood and revivify the principles of the religion." But the men insisted, "Do you bear witness that ʻUthmān was wrongfully killed?" "I would not say that," ʻAlī answered. They retorted, "We dissociate ourselves from anyone who does not so bear witness."[70]

The second is an alleged meeting between ʻAmmār b. Yāsir accompanied by a few noted supporters of ʻAlī and ʻAmr b. al-ʻĀṣ with a few notables from among Muʻāwiyah's supporters. ʻAmmār began by reminding ʻAmr that Muslims had been divided concerning ʻUthmān, with some deserting him and others calling for his death. Thus was he besieged in his house for forty days without leading a Friday prayer or holding any public assembly. Ṭalḥah and al-Zubayr, as well as ʻĀ'ishah, had first incited men to kill him, but when he was killed they rose up to demand retaliation for his blood. Likewise, Muʻāwiyah now championed ʻUthmān's cause, but in reality he only wanted ʻAlī to confirm his authority over Syria. ʻAmmār concluded, "Consider carefully this matter,

69. Ibn Muzāḥim, p. 200.
70. Ibid., pp. 201–202.

therefore; let the truth prevail over you and judge accordingly, be it for you or against you." ʿAmr agreed with ʿAmmār concerning ʿĀ'ishah, Ṭalḥah, and al-Zubayr, but insisted on Muʿāwiyah's right to demand retaliation for ʿUthmān's blood because of their close Umayyad kinship. He continued, "Why are you fighting us? Do we not all worship the one God? Do we not pray towards your direction [*qiblah*] of prayer, profess your faith, recite your Book and believe in your Prophet?" ʿAmmār angrily countered that only ʿAlī and his followers truly worshiped God, prayed, and recited the Qur'ān, while ʿAmr and his comrades were in manifest error. He went on:

> Do you not know that the Prophet said, "Anyone whose master (*mawlā*) I am, ʿAlī too is his master. O God, befriend those who befriend him and be an enemy to those who show enmity to him. Support those who support him and abandon those who abandon him."? I am an ally (*mawlā*) of God and His Messenger, and ʿAlī is my master (*mawlā*) after him. But as for you, you have no friend or master.[71]

This is the first time, to our knowledge, that this prophetic tradition, known as *ḥadīth al-Ghadīr*,[72] was directly cited as a proof-text in support of ʿAlī's right to the caliphate.

Ibn Muzāḥim presents a much sharper encounter between the two men. He reports that ʿAmr asked ʿAmmār directly, "What do you say concerning the killing of ʿUthmān?" ʿAmmār answered, "He [ʿUthmān] opened for you the door to every evil." ʿAmr asked further, "Was it ʿAlī then who killed him?" "No, it was God, the Lord of ʿAlī, and ʿAlī with Him, who killed him," retorted ʿAmmār. "Were you among those who killed him," asked ʿAmr. "Yes, I was with them, and today I am fighting along with them," was ʿAmmār's defiant reply. ʿAmr asked why they had killed ʿUthmān, and ʿAmmār answered, "He wished to alter our religion, so we killed him." ʿAmr turned to the men present and said, "Do you not hear? He has confessed to having killed ʿUthmān."[73]

71. al-Kūfī, vol. 3, pp. 123–125.
72. See Chapter 1, particularly the text immediately preceding and following note 4, p. 3.
73. Ibn Muzāḥim, p. 339.

It should be evident from our previous discussion of 'Uthmān's assassination and the events surrounding it that 'Ammār was not giving an account of who had actually killed 'Uthmān or why. Rather, he was expressing his dissatisfaction with 'Uthmān's rule and his anger at the harsh treatment he had received at the Caliph's hands and those of his Umayyad relatives. Indeed, the early Andalusian historian, traditionist, and belletrist Ibn 'Abd Rabbih reports that 'Alī was shocked and deeply dismayed at the news of 'Uthmān's death; that he sternly reprimanded his two sons Ḥasan and Ḥusayn for not having defended the Caliph; and, that he also closely questioned 'Uthmān's wife Nā'ilah, who had witnessed the event and lost some of her fingers trying to ward off the blows which had killed her husband. According to this account, it was Muḥammad b. Abū Bakr who brought into 'Uthmān's chamber two men who then killed him.[74]

It must therefore be concluded that the point at issue here was not the violent death of a pious Muslim, but the violation of the sanctity of caliphal authority. Hence, 'Uthmān's rule and death together provided the casus belli that sparked the conflict of Ṣiffīn. Furthermore, the Ṣiffīn civil war did not represent a conflict among different Arab tribes, but a clash between two religious, social, and political ideologies. It was a conflict between the caliphate as an old Arab and Islamic institution, represented by 'Alī, and an oligarchic rule, represented by Mu'āwiyah. The shift towards this new and unpopular form of government was initiated by 'Uthmān and developed into an autocratic authority by his Umayyad and 'Abbāsid successors. 'Alī's caliphate may therefore be regarded as a brief, but violent interruption of this inevitable development.

Throughout this period, tribal identity did continue to play an important role in the political affairs of the different regions of a rapidly growing Islamic dominion. However, tribal migration and settlement in major cities often led to the formation, in different regions, of different warring factions of one and the same tribe. The wrenching

74. Ibn 'Abd Rabbih, vol. 5. pp. 36–41.

consequences of such divisions are adequately illustrated in the following account of the tribe of Banū Khath'am, who were divided into the Khath'am of Syria and the Khath'am of Iraq – a split common to a number of major Arab tribes. In spite of their close kinship, they were not able to achieve peace amongst themselves. When, at Ṣiffīn, a man of the Syrian branch killed in single combat Abū Ka'b, the chief of the Khath'am of Iraq, he turned away weeping as he exclaimed, "May God have mercy on you, O Abū Ka'b, for I have killed you in obedience to certain people than whom you are much nearer to me in kinship and much dearer. By God, I know not what to say, for I see that Satan has indeed beguiled us, and that the men of the Quraysh have manipulated us."[75]

Beyond questions of tribal allegiance, many on both sides of the Ṣiffīn conflict were committed to moral and religious positions which they were not prepared to compromise. As we have seen, some men in Mu'āwiyah's camp were convinced that 'Uthmān had been wrongfully killed and that therefore, in accordance with the Qur'ān, his blood had to be requited (see Q.17:33). There were, on the other hand, many in 'Alī's camp who were equally convinced that 'Uthmān's death had been justified, and that to rise up against 'Alī, whom they regarded as a legitimately appointed caliph, was a serious violation of the Qur'ānic command, "[O]bey God and obey the Messenger and those of you who are in authority" (Q.4:59).

Furthermore, tribal loyalty and religious commitment were not mutually exclusive spheres. For these men, the order to fight and kill fellow Muslims with whom a close blood kinship existed – in violation of the Qur'ānic precept of showing kindness to a next-of-kin – was as grave a transgression as defying the command to obey those in authority by refusing to fight. This dilemma troubled many religiously minded men with regard to the conflicts of both the Camel and Ṣiffīn. Their distress is dramatically expressed by a man of the tribe of the Banū Asad of Iraq as he faced in battle his Syrian kinsmen:

75. Ibn Muzāḥim, p. 257.

> It is indeed a great calamity that we have been turned against our own people and they have been turned against us. For, by God, it is only our hands with which we cut off our own hands . . . If we do not fight, we shall not be sincere in our loyalty to our ally ['Alī], nor would we stand by our brethren. But if we do, it is our own dignity that we violate and our fire that we extinguish.[76]

Not all those present at Ṣiffīn were concerned with political ideologies or religious values. Many of the fighters on both sides were motivated either by the pre-Islamic zeal (*ḥamiyyah*) to preserve tribal honor at any cost, or by the prospect of wealth and booty. Men from each camp would meet between the lines of battle to recite pre-Islamic panegyrics boasting of the high prestige and noble lineage of their tribal ancestors. Driven by this tribal zeal, Ibn Muzāḥim observes, "they steadfastly stood their ground, being so ashamed of running away that war nearly consumed them."[77]

At Ṣiffīn, not only did Muslims kill Muslims, but often a man killed his brother or cousin. In many respects, this tragic civil war resembled the intertribal feuds of pre-Islamic times, when neither marriage ties nor blood relations deterred men from exacting revenge on one another. Ṣiffīn degenerated from a battle fought over religious and moral commitments or political and personal ambitions to war-cries of tribal and genealogical boasting. Thus, when a man of the tribe of Tamīm, in 'Alī's camp, saw his kinsmen run away, he called them back to battle with the slogans of tribal solidarity (*ḥamiyyah*) of the time of *jāhiliyyah*. To the objection of some of the men of his tribe, that it was unlawful for him to use such war-cries, he answered, "Alas for you, running away is far worse, for if you will not fight for the cause of your religion and the certainty of your faith, then at least fight for the cause of preserving your genealogical dignity."[78] The man himself fought valiantly until he died.

Soon after the Muḥarram truce ended, the single combat

76. Ibid., p. 262.
77. Ibid., p. 332.
78. Ibid., p. 265.

skirmishes, which had initiated the conflict of Ṣiffīn, turned into a full scale war and many lives were lost on both sides. The war was clearly going in 'Ali's favor, which greatly alarmed Mu'āwiyah. He too resorted to the old war tactics of pre-Islamic chivalrous tribal solidarity. He is reported to have called together the men of the Quraysh, in the dead of night, and reproached them for their lack of bravery, saying:

> I marvel at you, O men of the Quraysh, for no one of you will have a tale with which to draw out his song tomorrow and say such and such were my great feats at Ṣiffīn. I have not seen anyone of you who went out to do battle with these people but that he returned in disgrace. Is this how victory over 'Alī can be won? By God, they are defending 'Alī with their lives and he too is ready to defend them with his life.[79]

Marwān b. al-Ḥakam replied, "You have spoken; listen now to the answer. How can we boast over them when their pride is righteousness?" If they were to boast with Umayyad past power and prestige, Marwān argued, then past dominion belonged to the tribes of the Yaman, not to the tribe of the Quraysh. Even if, on the other hand, they were to boast with their Qurayshite lineage, then the Arabs had all accorded the house of 'Abd al-Muṭṭalib honor and prestige, and 'Alī was of that house. Marwān concluded, "With what would you then boast over him?"[80]

Ibn Muzāḥim relates that Mu'āwiyah gave generous stipends to the men of the Yamanite tribe of 'Akk, for which alone they agreed to fight. The men of Iraq coveted such rich gifts and therefore greedily turned their gaze towards Mu'āwiyah. This was because 'Alī would not violate his principle of equity in the distribution of wealth, even in times of war. Sensing this, Mu'āwiyah vowed to buy 'Alī's most trusted men saying, "By God, I will distribute wealth so abundantly among them that my world shall overcome their hereafter."[81]

As Mu'āwiyah's situation became more critical, he sent a group of

79. al-Kūfī, vol. 3, pp. 175–176.
80. Ibid., p. 176.
81. Ibn Muzāḥim, p. 453.

men with ʿAmr b. al-ʿAṣ and Shurḥabīl b. al-Ṣamt to negotiate a truce with ʿAlī. Shurḥabīl argued that the people of Syria and Iraq were bound by close blood kinship as well as ties of intermarriage. After speaking laudatorily of ʿAlī's close kinship with the Prophet and his priority in Islam, and his bravery, nobility, and honor, Shurḥabīl went on, "God knows and you know that we have fought one another with the zeal (*ḥamiyyah*) of pre-Islamic folly (*jāhiliyyah*), and with sharp Indian swords." Shurḥabīl then warned ʿAlī that, if the war went on any longer, the Byzantines would turn against the men of Syria, kill them, and enslave their women and children, and the Persians would do the same to the people of Iraq. He continued, "We therefore think it best that you, O Abū al-Ḥasan, depart with your men, so that we leave you to your Ḥijāz and Iraq and you leave us to our Syria. Thus would we stop the shedding of the blood of Muslims."[82]

ʿAlī of course, could not agree to a plan that would mean the dismemberment of the Islamic state and the destruction of the caliphal office. He was, nonetheless, greatly disturbed by the reality of Muslims shedding the blood of Muslims. He said, "By God, I have so thoroughly considered this matter . . . that it has deprived me of sleep. I find no choice but for me to either fight you or reject faith in what Muḥammad brought [from God]." ʿAlī then suggested that he and Muʿāwiyah meet alone and that each of them invoke God's curse on the other and pray that God help the one in the right to kill the one in the wrong.[83] Then they would engage in a duel, and whoever of them killed the other would be unanimously acclaimed as leader. "By God," he concluded, "no one fights on Muʿāwiyah's side but that God will cast him headlong into the fire of Hell."[84]

Despite ʿAlī's sharp rebuff of Muʿāwiyah's emissaries, Muʿāwiyah

82. al-Kūfī, vol. 3, p. 286.
83. The practice of imprecation known as *mubāhalah* or *mulāʿanah* is an ancient Arab custom, which Islam confirmed. God commanded the Prophet in the Qur'ān (3:61) to call the delegation of the Christians of Najrān to a *mubāhalah*, or mutual invocation of a Divine curse. See M. Ayoub, *The Qur'ān*, vol. 2, pp. 188–202.
84. al-Kūfī, vol. 3, pp. 286–287; see also Ibn Muzāḥim, p. 475.

wrote to him arguing that had they known the dire consequences the war would have for both parties, neither would have engaged in it in the first place. Still, he argued, there was time to repair the great damage it had caused. He then suggested a way out:

> I asked you before to cede Syria to me and to accept that I owe you neither allegiance nor obedience, but you refused. God has, however, granted me what you withheld. I call you today to what I called you yesterday . . . Furthermore, we are both descendants of 'Abd Manāf. Neither of us therefore can claim priority over the other except in that through which no honourable man could be disgraced or free man enslaved [i.e. Islam].[85]

'Alī's answer is specially significant in that it expresses, once more, his uncompromising idealism as well as the popular view of the socio-religious qualifications for the caliphate. He does not directly refer to Mu'āwiyah's request, but instead affirms his determination not to compromise his God-given authority: "Were I to be killed in the way of God then revived then killed and revived seventy times, I would not turn away from my unyielding strictness in His cause and the duty to strive against His enemies." With regard to their common ancestry, 'Alī said:

> We are indeed sons of one father. Yet Umayyah is not like Hāshim, nor is Ḥarb [Mu'āwiyah's grandfather] like 'Abd al-Muṭṭalib ['Alī's grandfather], or Abū Sufyān like Abū Ṭālib. Nor is the Immigrant (*muhājir*) the same as he who was pardoned (*ṭalīq*),[86] or he who is in the right like he who is in the wrong. We, moreover [the house of Hāshim], possess the honor of Prophethood by means of which we abased the mighty and exalted the humble.[87]

Abū Sufyān and his family accepted Islam under constraint, just before the conquest of Makkah, hence they were among those who received special pardon from the Prophet. This rendered them unfit

85. Ibn Muzāḥim, pp. 474–475.
86. The first generation of Muslims following the death of the Prophet were religiously, and hence socially, divided into three categories: *al-muhājirūn* (the Immigrants); *al-anṣār* (the Supporters); and, *al-ṭulaqā'* [pl. of *ṭalīq*], those who accepted Islam at the last minute and were pardoned by the Prophet on the day of the conquest of Makkah.
87. Ibn Muzāḥim, p. 471; see also Ibn Qutaybah, vol. 1, p. 138.

for the caliphate, and thus they were not included in any consultative or decision-making company.[88]

It may be inferred from our discussion so far that to call the conflict of Ṣiffīn a "battle" (*waq'ah*), as is generally done in our classical sources, is a misnomer. The reason for this mistaken designation is that Arab warfare, until the rise of the caliphate, consisted of single raids or battles (*ghazawāt*) that usually lasted no more than a day and ended inconclusively – their primary aim being booty, prestige, or vendetta. In contrast, the "Battle of Ṣiffīn" was the first sustained civil war under Islam. As this war went on and the number of casualties dramatically mounted, calls for a truce were increasingly voiced in both camps. These calls for an end to the fighting, in reality, admitted of an inconclusive end to the greater conflict between 'Alī and Mu'āwiyah.

The fighting finally reached a climax on Ṣafar 11, A.H. 37 (July 28, 657), known as the "day of growling" (*yawm al-harīr*), when 'Alī clearly had the upper hand. On that night he assessed the situation as follows: "O people, you see for yourselves your own state and that of your enemies; they are at their last breath." He then declared his intention: "I shall advance against them early tomorrow morning and bring them to God's judgment."[89]

On the same night, Mu'āwiyah called on 'Amr for advice. 'Amr began by praising the valor of 'Alī and his men and deprecating Mu'āwiyah and his soldiers for their lack of purpose and probity:

> Your men cannot withstand his men, nor are you like him. 'Alī is fighting you over one principle, and you are fighting him over another. You desire life, but he desires death. Furthermore, the people of Iraq will be afraid of you if you conquer them, while the people of Syria will not be afraid of 'Alī if he conquers them.

'Amr then revealed his masterful war stratagem. "Present them," he advised, "with a proposal that will cause dissension among them

88. This point is poignantly made by Ibn 'Abbās in answer to a letter from Mu'āwiyah urging him to desert 'Alī and nominate himself for the caliphate. See Ibn Muzāḥim, p. 415. See also p. 94, note 32.
89. Ibn Muzāḥim, p. 476.

whether they accept or reject it. Call them to the Book of God as an arbiter between us and them." 'Amr added, "I have kept this scheme a well-guarded secret for the time when you would need it most."[90]

'Amr's Scheme and its Consequences

It is probable that the fighting at Ṣiffīn would have stopped in any case, as men on both sides were becoming increasingly convinced of its danger and futility. 'Amr's scheme appears to have had other and far more serious aims than simple disengagement. It was meant not only to bring a stop to the fighting, but to create disunity in 'Alī's camp. More importantly, it was aimed at compromising 'Alī's caliphal authority by placing Mu'āwiyah on an equal footing with him. The ultimate goal was to revoke 'Alī's caliphate in favor of either Mu'āwiyah or another man more amenable to the Qurayshite aristocracy. As we shall see, 'Amr's scheme met with great success on all counts.

'Amr directed that copies of the Qur'ān be immediately lifted up on the tips of spears and that criers be sent out to call on 'Alī's men to cease fighting and let the Book of God decide between them. Thus copies, or more likely leaves, of the Qur'ān were raised up high and criers exclaimed with a loud voice: "O men of the Arabs! In God's name! who will protect your wives and daughters? Who will face the Byzantines, the Turks, and the Persians tomorrow if you perish? In God's name, beware! It is your religion! Here is the Book of God between us and you." Hearing this, 'Alī said, "O God, You surely know that it is not the Book that they want. Judge, therefore, between us and them."[91]

It should be noted that any religious issues the Ṣiffīn conflict may have raised were, in the end, overshadowed by practical, personal, and tribal interests. As we saw, everyone in Mu'āwiyah's camp wanted the war to end, not for any religious or moral reasons, but because they

90. Ibid.

91. Ibid., p. 478. For different versions of this report, see al-Ya'qūbī, vol. 2, pp. 189–190; al-Kūfī, vol. 3, pp. 305 ff.; Ibn Qutaybah, vol. 1, p. 101; and, Ibn Abī al-Ḥadīd, vol. 2, p. 210.

were losing it. 'Alī's camp was divided into several factions. The majority wanted a truce, as they were growing weary of such a long and bloody war whose consequences they greatly feared. A small minority, quite certain of victory, wished to see the war through to its bitter end. Finally, a few argued for obedience to 'Alī and the obligation to abide by his judgment as the legitimate imām of the Muslims, regardless of the consequences.

The first faction was further divided into two camps, with the majority arguing for answering the call to let the Book of God judge between the opposing armies. Others argued for an immediate end to hostilities at any cost; they were convinced that the war threatened the very existence of the Arabs and their Arabo-Islamic state. The chief spokesman for all those who vied for a truce was al-Ash'ath b. Qays al-Kindī, while the chief advocate for those who wished to bring the war to a conclusive end was Mālik al-Ashtar al-Nakh'ī. It is noteworthy that although the two men were of Yamanite stock, they took completely opposite positions on this important issue.

Al-Ash'ath was a man of advanced age and pragmatic disposition. He began his impassioned appeal for the fighting to stop by observing that, in spite of his old age, he had never seen so much bloodshed in one day. He then warned, "If we face each other again tomorrow, it shall be the annihilation of the Arabs and the violation of all inviolable sanctions." He concluded by asserting that he did not speak out of fear of death, rather, he said, "I fear for the safety of women and children if we perish."[92]

In answer to the entreaties of al-Ash'ath, 'Abd Allāh, son of 'Amr b. al-'Āṣ, and other well-meaning men in both camps, pleas for a cessation of hostilities and peace negotiations were earnestly made. A large number of 'Alī's soldiers demanded that he accept the call of Mu'āwiyah and his men to let the Book of God judge between them. They threatened, "O 'Alī, answer the call of the people to the Book of God, or we shall kill you as we killed 'Uthmān b. 'Affān. By God, we

92. Ibn Muzāḥim, pp. 480–481.

shall do it if you do not heed their call." ʿAlī cautioned them not to be deceived by this seemingly pious act. He said, "It is a word of truth [they utter], but they intend only falsehood by it." He begged them to fight on for only another hour, as victory was so near at hand, but they absolutely refused. In desperation he concluded, "I have indeed been fighting them in order that they abide by the judgment of the Qur'ān . . . I have informed you that they have deceived you, for it is not abiding by the Qur'ān that they desire."[93]

These dissenters were pious men who spent their nights in prayer and recitation of the Qur'ān. Their uncompromising piety, however, was combined with intractable individualism and strict egalitarianism. They were not, moreover, just a few hard-headed men, but thousands of brave and persuasive warriors. Within a short time they would come to be a cohesive opposition not only to ʿAlī, but to the whole caliphal establishment. Hence, they earned the appellation "*khawārij*" (Kharijites), "those who went out," that is, of ʿAlī's camp. In reality, they seceded from the Muslim *ummah* altogether.

Ibn Aʿtham al-Kūfī's report of this encounter suggests that ʿAlī was, in the end, persuaded by the reasoning of these dissenters. This is not improbable, as he essentially shared their uncompromising position with regard to religious obligations and commitments. He was also challenged by the call itself, which he could not refuse. ʿAlī said:

> O people, surely beside the Book of God there is no command, nor is there beside its judgment any judgment. Behold, the people have called us to the Book of God, and I love to revivify what the Qur'ān has revived and to abolish what the Qur'ān has abolished. You know well that we were with the Messenger of God on the day of Ḥudaybiyyah when we wanted to fight in opposition to the truce, but he forbade us. Now the people of Syria have called us to the Book of God under constraint, but we will answer them with clemency.[94]

Ibn Muzāḥim reports that the Kharijites then demanded that ʿAlī recall al-Ashtar from the battlefield, just as the latter was about to

93. Ibid., pp. 489–490.
94. al-Kūfī, vol. 3, p. 317.

enter Mu'āwiyah's quarters. Al-Ashtar returned reluctantly and in vain begged them to allow him only the time "of a horse's gallop," as he was certain of a quick victory. But they insisted, "We have fought them in God's cause, and we shall cease fighting them for God's sake." Al-Ashtar's harsh reproach of the Kharijites expresses well the contempt with which Muslims in general have held that movement. He said, "O men of blackened foreheads [that is from constant prostration], we thought that your ardent prayers were an expression of your renunciation of the world and your longing for meeting with God. I see instead that you are running away from death to the life of this world."[95] The men became so incensed that they began beating one another with their horse whips. Fearing sedition and the outbreak of a more serious conflict, 'Alī ordered them to stop. This was misinterpreted as a willingness on 'Alī's part to end the fighting altogether. Thus, the rumor that he had accepted arbitration quickly spread.

Mu'āwiyah then sent a deputy to ask 'Alī for a truce and a stop to the shedding of blood. After much hesitation, 'Alī answered, "We have answered, not the call to your judgment, but the call to the judgment of the Qur'ān, for whoever refused the judgment of the Qur'ān would stray far from the right course."[96] Mu'āwiyah's deputy was Abū al-A'war al-Sulamī, an astute pro-Umayyad negotiator. Al-Ash'ath, who was far more committed to stopping the fighting than to 'Alī's cause, eagerly volunteered to negotiate with Mu'āwiyah on 'Alī's behalf.[97]

It was agreed that two arbiters be chosen, one representing Mu'āwiyah and the people of Syria, the other representing 'Alī and the people of Iraq. Mu'āwiyah and his men quickly nominated 'Amr b. al-'Āṣ. 'Alī's men, after much wrangling, chose Abū Mūsā al-Ash'arī. 'Alī rejected Abū Mūsa because, when Abū Mūsā was governor of Kūfah, he had opposed the Battle of the Camel and sought to turn people against 'Alī. 'Alī then suggested Ibn 'Abbās, but al-Ash'ath and

95. Ibn Muzāḥim, p. 491.
96. Ibid., pp. 493–494.
97. Ibid.; and al-Kūfī, vol. 3, pp. 320–325.

his fellow Yamanite tribesmen rejected him. He then suggested al-Ashtar, but al-Ash'ath objected on the ground that al-Ashtar always worked against their efforts to stop the bloodshed. He added, "Are we not under his judgment, anyhow?" 'Alī asked, "And what is his judgment?" Al-Ash'ath answered, "His judgment is that we strike one another with swords until you and he get what you want."[98]

An equally sharp interchange between 'Alī and al-Ash'ath is reported on the authority of 'Alī's great-great-grandson, the fifth Shī'ī Imām, Muḥammad al-Bāqir. 'Alī, according to this account, argued that Mu'āwiyah could not have found anyone more capable of negotiating on his behalf than was 'Amr b. al-'Āṣ. Therefore, he continued, only a capable man of the Quraysh, one who was the equal of 'Amr, could stand up to him and negotiate successfully. 'Alī declared that Ibn 'Abbās, alone, was a match for 'Amr. But al-Ash'ath objected, "No by God, no two men of Muḍar will be allowed to lord over us until the Day of Resurrection!" He insisted that, since the men of Syria had chosen a Muḍarite, 'Alī had to appoint a Yamanite to counterbalance him. In vain 'Alī cautioned, "I am afraid that your Yamanite will be deceived by their Muḍarite, for 'Amr has no scruples and cares little about God when he desires a thing."[99] 'Alī eventually conceded, and Abū Mūsā al-Ash'arī was named as negotiator.

In contrast with 'Amr b. al-'Āṣ, who was unreservedly committed to Mu'āwiyah's cause, Abū Mūsā was an unwilling arbiter who cared little for either 'Alī or Mu'āwiyah. During the Ṣiffīn conflict, he abandoned his post as governor of Kūfah and chose to live in the desert, far from the fighting. When he was told that the people had reached a peace agreement, he exclaimed, "Praise be to God, Lord of all beings" (Q.1:2). But when he was further informed that he had been made an arbiter between 'Alī and Mu'āwiyah, he sadly said, "Surely, to God we belong, and to Him we will return" (Q.2:156).[100] Even before the start

98. Ibn Muzāḥim, p. 499.
99. Ibid., p. 499; al-Kūfī, vol. 4, pp. 1–4.
100. Ibn Muzāḥim, p. 500. This verse is usually repeated at the news of death or serious calamity.

of the arbitration process, Abū Mūsā's attitude placed 'Alī at a definite disadvantage. In fact, 'Alī had already compromised his own authority by accepting arbitration in the first place, regardless of the outcome.

'Alī's precarious position can be clearly discerned in the controversy surrounding the drafting of the document of arbitration. As the ruling caliph, 'Alī began to dictate the truce conditions saying, "This is what 'Alī, Commander of the Faithful, and Mu'āwiyah b. Abī Sufyān have agreed upon." But Mu'āwiyah angrily returned the document to 'Alī's amanuensis with the retort, "I would indeed be a foolish man if I were to acknowledge him as the Commander of the Faithful and then fight him." And 'Amr declared, "Rather, write his name and his father's name, for he is your commander only; our commander, he is not!" When the document was returned to 'Alī he directed that the phrase "Commander of the Faithful" be deleted. Al-Aḥnaf b. Qays, one of his devoted followers, cautioned, "Do not efface the title of Commander from yourself. For, I fear that if you efface it, it shall never be restored to you. Do not efface it, even if the people kill each other."[101] 'Alī hesitated until al-Ash'ath came and insisted that he comply with Mu'āwiyah's demand. 'Alī observed as he deleted his title, that he himself had deleted the title "Messenger of God" for the Prophet from the document of the truce of Ḥudaybiyyah at the insistence of Abū Sufyān, and that now he did the same thing at the behest of Abū Sufyān's son.[102]

The Ṣiffīn truce agreement was a pious but ineffectual document that lacked any real political or military substance. It was therefore ignored by both arbiters. However, the phrasing and very existence of this agreement resulted in 'Alī's loss of both the war and the caliphate. Some of the salient clauses are:

101. Ibid., p. 506.
102. al-Kūfī, vol. 4, pp. 8–9; Ibn Abī al-Ḥadīd, vol. 2, p. 232. In fact Abū Sufyān was not even present at Ḥudaybiyyah. For the controversy surrounding the Ḥudaybiyyah document and 'Alī's role in it, see Alfred Guillaume, *The Life of Muḥammad, Translation of Ibn Isaq's Sīrat Rasūl Allāh*, 2nd edn. (Lahore: Oxford University Press, 1968), pp. 499–507.

1. Both ʻAlī and Muʻāwiyah and with them the peoples of Iraq and Syria shall accept the arbitration of the Qur'ān and abide by its judgment;
2. ʻAlī and his party (*shīʻah*) will appoint ʻAbd Allāh b. Qays Abū Mūsā al-Ashʻarī as their arbiter, and Muʻāwiyah and his party will appoint ʻAmr b. al-ʻA¯ṣ as their arbiter, and the two men shall be bound by God's covenant to take the Qur'ān as their sole guide (*imām*) in their deliberations;
3. If they do not find what they seek in the Qur'ān, they will seek it in the uniting, and not the dividing, *sunnah* of the Prophet,
4. ʻAmr and ʻAbd Allāh will bind both ʻAlī and Muʻāwiyah by God's covenant to accept their arbitration, and the Muslim *ummah* shall stand by them and guarantee their safety and the inviolability of their blood, property and families.[103]

It should be stressed that this document treats ʻAlī and Muʻāwiyah not as ruler and insurgent, but as two equal contenders. It refers to them as the "two *amīrs*" (chiefs) and to their two deputies as the two arbiters, "*ḥakamayn*." It thus implicitly denies ʻAlī's caliphal prerogative. The two arbiters are given a year to reach an acceptable verdict. If, however, they were to fail to come to a decision within the stipulated time, then things would be as before, and the state of war would be resumed.

Having affixed the seals of both ʻAlī and Muʻāwiyah to the document, al-Ashʻath went around the two camps to read it aloud to the different tribes. When the men of the tribe of Banū ʻAnzah heard the document, two of their young men, who were brothers, exclaimed, "Judgment, or arbitration [*ḥukm*] belongs to God alone!" They were the first to voice this categorical rejection of arbitration. They then took up their swords and launched an attack on the Syrian camp and fought until they were killed near the entrance to Muʻāwiyah's quarters.[104]

The slogan "No judgment but God's judgment" quickly spread through ʻAlī's camp. It expressed the dissatisfaction of the elders of the various tribes and their fighters with a war that had claimed so many lives, but achieved nothing. It expressed, as well, their rejection of a

103. Ibn Muzāḥim, pp. 505–506. For a full text of this document see Appendix II below.
104. Ibid., p. 512.

truce agreement that compromised the authority of God and His Prophet, represented by a legitimate imām of all the Muslims. Some of the men of the tribes of Rāsib and Tamīm, who became staunch Kharijites, declared, "No judgment but God's judgment. We do not accept the arbitration of men in God's religion!" One of their spokesmen, 'Urwah b. Udiyah, a prominent Kharijite, reproached al-Ash'ath, "Where then are our fallen men, O Ash'ath?" Much uproar ensued, as many loudly cried out:

> Judgment belongs to God, O 'Alī, not to you. We shall not accept to have men arbitrate in the religion of God. God has already passed judgment on Mu'āwiyah and his men: either they submit to our judgment over them or they will be killed. We sinned and erred when we accepted arbitration. Now that our sin and error have become clear to us, we turn to God and repent. Turn to God and repent as we have done, or we will dissociate ourselves from you.

'Alī answered, "Shall we turn back after accepting arbitration and binding ourselves with a strict covenant?"[105]

The two arbiters met in Dawmat al-Jandal, a spot midway between Syria and Iraq. 'Alī sent Abū Mūsā with four hundred men and Ibn 'Abbās as prayer leader, and Mu'āwiyah sent an equal number of men with 'Amr b. al-'Āṣ. While the two men appear to have conducted most of their deliberations privately, they were not alone. Many curious men, in fact, frequented their meetings to offer advice or collect news for the chiefs of the two contending camps. Historians and traditionists present different accounts of the details of these deliberations. They are, however, in full agreement regarding the outcome.

As the two arbiters spent days and weeks in fruitless negotiations, the people on both sides grew restless and rumors spread. 'Amr and Abū Mūsā could not come to an agreement because each had a different perception of the problem, and each had his own solution for it. It was rumored that 'Amr wanted the caliphate for himself or his son, while Abū Mūsā wanted a man who had had no part in the conflict. He

105. Ibn Abī al-Ḥadīd, vol. 2, p. 240, and Ibn Muzāḥim, pp. 513–514.

thus preferred ʿAbd Allāh b. ʿUmar b. al-Khaṭṭāb who, as we saw, had chosen not to take sides with either ʿAlī or Muʿāwiyah.

Muʿāwiyah sent al-Mughīrah b. Shuʿbah to assess the situation and bring him news of what was actually taking place. Al-Mughīrah asked Abū Mūsā, "What would you say concerning those who stayed out of this affair and abhorred all this bloodshed, so that they were neither with ʿAlī nor with Muʿāwiyah?" He answered, "These, by God, are among the best of those whose backs were relieved of the burden of the wrongs suffered by God's worshipful servants." Al-Mughīrah then put the same question to ʿAmr, who said, "These are among the most wicked of God's creatures, for they neither upheld a truth nor repudiated a falsehood."[106] Al-Mughīrah's assessment was that Abū Mūsā would remove ʿAlī from the caliphate and direct that it be conferred upon a man who had not been involved in the conflict, and that his inclination was for ʿAbd Allāh b. ʿUmar. "As for ʿAmr," al-Mughīrah continued, "he remains the friend you know."[107]

As negotiations reached a dead end, ʿAmr again resorted to clever subterfuge. He first tried to convince Abū Mūsā to nominate Muʿāwiyah for the caliphate on the grounds of his honored status in the Quraysh, his companionship (*ṣuḥbah*) with the Prophet and the fact that he was the brother of Umm Ḥabībah, one of the Prophet's wives. But Abū Mūsā argued that the caliphal office should be conferred on the basis not of honor, but of righteous conduct and moral probity. He continued, "Were I to confer the caliphate on the most highly honored man of the Quraysh, I would grant it to ʿAlī Ibn Abī Ṭālib."[108]

ʿAmr then promised Abū Mūsā that, if he were to side with Muʿāwiyah, the latter would reward him with the governorship of any province he wished; again, Abū Mūsā refused. ʿAmr then asked him in the presence of a large gathering, "Do you know that ʿUthmān was wrongfully killed?" "Yes," Abū Mūsā answered. ʿAmr turned to the men

106. al-Kūfī, vol. 4, pp. 26–27; see also al-Ṭabarī, vol. 5, pp. 57–58.
107. Ibn Muzāḥim, p. 540.
108. al-Ṭabarī, vol. 5, p. 68.

and said, "Bear witness." He then asked Abū Mūsā whether he believed Mu'āwiyah to be one of 'Uthmān's blood heirs, and Abū Mūsā agreed. "What prevents you," 'Amr asked, "from nominating Mu'āwiyah for the caliphate?" 'Amr counselled Abū Mūsā to say, if people questioned the wisdom of such a decision, "I found Mu'āwiyah to be 'Uthmān's heir and the one with the right to demand retaliation for his blood." He added that Abū Mūsā could also argue that he found Mu'āwiyah to be "a wise politician and an able governor."[109]

Abū Mūsā, however, was adamant in his rejection of Mu'āwiyah. He first suggested that they depose both 'Alī and Mu'āwiyah and appoint as caliph 'Abd Allāh b. 'Umar, because he had stayed out of the conflict altogether. 'Amr objected, "This office requires a man with a strong tooth who knows how to eat himself and how to feed others, and 'Abd Allāh is not such a man."[110] Finally the two men agreed to depose 'Alī and Mu'āwiyah and call for the election of a new caliph through general consultation.

They then came before a large gathering who anxiously awaited their verdict. Abū Mūsā announced that he and 'Amr had come to a decision that, they hoped, would bring peace and concord to the *ummah*. 'Amr concurred and called on him to speak. Ibn 'Abbās warned Abū Mūsā that 'Amr meant to trick him. If they had actually come to an agreement, Ibn 'Abbās cautioned, "Let 'Amr speak first." Abū Mūsā, however, stepped forward and said:

> My companion and I have agreed to remove both 'Alī and Mu'āwiyah and face anew this matter through general consultation among the Muslims, so that they may appoint anyone they choose to manage their affairs. I therefore depose both 'Alī and Mu'āwiyah. Take charge of this matter yourselves and bestow the caliphate on whomever you deem worthy of it.

'Amr then arose and said:

> You have all heard what this man has said, and that he has deposed his companion. I too depose him as he did, and confirm my companion

109. Ibn Muzāḥim, p. 541.
110. Ibid.

> Mu'āwiyah in the caliphate. This is because he is 'Uthmān's heir and requiter of his blood, and therefore most worthy of his station.

Abū Mūsā retorted angrily, "What is the matter with you, may God not aid you! You have acted wickedly and treacherously; you are 'like a dog, if you scold him he pants and if you leave him he pants' (Q.7:176)." 'Amr sarcastically retorted, "You are like 'a donkey loaded with scrolls' (Q. 62:5)."[111]

Ibn A'tham al-Kūfī, who claims to base his story of the Battle of Ṣiffīn largely on Ibn Muzāḥim's report,[112] presents a significantly different account of the episode under consideration. He states that 'Amr himself suggested they depose 'Alī and Mu'āwiyah and nominate instead 'Abd Allāh b. 'Umar as caliph. When, however, they came before the people to announce their decision, 'Amr asked Abū Mūsā, in the presence of witnesses brought there for the purpose, "I adjure you by God, who is more worthy of this office, he who acted honourably or he who acted treacherously?" "No," Abū Mūsā answered, "rather he who acted honourably." 'Amr went on, "What do you say concerning 'Uthmān, was he killed as a wrongdoer or as one who was wronged?" "Rather, as one who was wronged," Abū Mūsā answered. 'Amr then asked whether 'Uthmān's murderer should or should not be killed in retaliation for his blood, and Abū Mūsā agreed that he should be killed. 'Amr questioned Abū Mūsā further as to who had the right to kill 'Uthmān's murderer. Abū Mūsā replied that in accordance with the Qur'ānic ruling (Q.17:33) it should be his heirs. 'Amr finally asked, "Do you know that Mu'āwiyah is one of 'Uthmān's heirs?" Abū Mūsā agreed that he indeed was. 'Amr then turned to the witnesses and said, "Bear witness to what Abū Mūsā has just said." Abū Mūsā turned to them and declared, "Yes, bear witness to what I say: Mu'āwiyah is indeed one of 'Uthmān's blood heirs."[113]

111. Ibid., pp. 545–546.
112. See al-Kūfī, vol. 3, p. 344.
113. Ibid., vol. 4, pp. 28–30.

Abū Mūsā then called on 'Amr to rise and depose Mu'āwiyah, as they had agreed the day before. But 'Amr insisted that Abū Mūsā speak first because, he said, "God has placed you ahead of me in faith [*imān*] and migration [*hijrah*]." Abū Mūsā then rose and declared:

> O people, surely the best of men is he who is good to himself and the most wicked is he who is evil towards himself. You know full well that these wars [i.e., the Camel and Ṣiffīn] have spared neither the righteous and the God-fearing, nor the one in the right, nor the one in the wrong. I have, therefore, after careful consideration, decided that we should depose both 'Alī and Mu'āwiyah and appoint for this affair 'Abd Allāh b. 'Umar b. al-Khaṭṭāb, for he has neither stretched a hand nor drawn a tongue in these wars. Behold, I shall remove 'Alī from the caliphate as I now remove my ring from my finger.

Then 'Amr rose and said:

> Behold, this is 'Abd Allāh b. Qays Abū Mūsā al-Ash'arī, the deputy of the people of Yaman to the Messenger of God and representative of 'Umar b. al-Khaṭṭāb and the arbiter of the people of Iraq; he has removed his companion 'Alī from the caliphate. As for me, I confirm Mu'āwiyah in the caliphate as firmly as this ring sits around my finger.[114]

The Collapse of 'Alī's Rule and the End of the Normative Caliphate

The inconclusive end to arbitration, and hence to the conflict of Ṣiffīn, created a power-vacuum. With hitherto unprecedented force and political cunning, Mu'āwiyah quickly moved to fill it. 'Alī, the great warrior, has the distinction of having never lost an armed battle. But 'Alī, the man of unshakable ideals, lost the battle for his political credibility and caliphal authority to unscrupulous men who shared neither his piety nor his idealism.

To recapitulate, several factors contributed to 'Alī's tragic end. First, the spectre of 'Uthmān's assassination continued to haunt his caliphate until his death. Second, 'Alī's involvement in the first bloody civil conflicts in Muslim history turned many genuine Muslims away

114. Ibid., pp. 29–31. See also al-Ṭabarī, vol. 5, pp. 70–71.

from him and, in the end, cost him both his political and moral authority. Third, as has already been demonstrated, while 'Alī's uncompromising uprightness in the management of state affairs and his strict equity in the distribution of wealth made him a paragon of justice and righteous conduct, it nonetheless deprived him of the support and loyalty of the majority of his Arab subjects, particularly the men of the Quraysh. All three factors can be clearly discerned in 'Alī's repeatedly futile attempts to recover his political authority after Ṣiffīn.

It was argued above that 'Alī was not directly involved in 'Uthmān's assassination. But the fact that he may have thought it justified, and hence did little to prevent it or to take any measures to punish its perpetrators, made him, in the eyes of many of the Prophet's companions, in some way responsible for the violent death of the imām of the Muslims. Furthermore, the ensuing bloody conflicts between 'Alī and the Quraysh aristocracy on the one hand, and between him and some of his staunch but disaffected supporters on the other, were regarded by many as divisive consequences of this heinous act. This view is clearly expressed in a telling interchange between 'Alī and some notables of the Quraysh, who went to him after Ṣiffīn to demand their stipends. Among them were 'Abd Allāh b. 'Umar, Sa'd b. Abī Waqqāṣ and al-Mughīrah b. Shu'bah.

'Alī angrily asked, "What kept you away from me all this time?" "'Uthmān's assassination," they answered, "for we do not know whether his blood was lawful to shed or not." They continued:

> Certainly, 'Uthmān did commit improprieties, but you ['Alī and his supporters] made him repent and he did. Still, you were involved in his death when he was killed. We do not know whether you did the right thing or not. We, of course, fully acknowledge your excellence, priority [in Islam] and migration (*hijrah*), O Commander of the Faithful.

'Alī reminded them of the Qur'ānic dictum "If two parties of the Muslims fight one another, fight the one that transgresses until it submits to God's command" (Q.49:9.). Thus he argued, "You did not enjoin the good, as God commanded." Sa'd answered, "O 'Alī, give me a sword that can distinguish the man of faith from the rejecter of faith.

I am afraid of killing a Muslim and thereby entering the Fire." But 'Alī responded that, if they knew 'Uthmān to have been a legitimate imām to whom obedience was due and if he was in the right, then why had they abandoned him? If, on the other hand, he was in the wrong, why had they not fought him? 'Alī concluded:

> If 'Uthmān was right in what he did, then you committed wrongdoing by not supporting your imām. But if he was in error, again you committed wrongdoing by not supporting those who sought to enjoin the good and dissuade from evil. In any case you committed wrongdoing by not intervening between us and our enemies as God commanded you to do, for He says, "Fight the one that transgresses until it submits to God's command."[115]

It was observed above that the people of Syria considered Mu'āwiyah as their sole ruler even before the conflict of Ṣiffīn.[116] Thus, when he returned to Damascus after 'Amr had confirmed him as successor to 'Uthmān, they saluted him as the Caliph.[117] Moreover, the Yamanite pro-'Uthmān party rose up against 'Alī's governor 'Ubayd Allāh b. 'Abbās demanding requital for 'Uthmān's blood. They wrote to Mu'āwiyah asking him to send someone to receive their *bay'ah*; otherwise, they would apologize to 'Alī for their misdeeds and pledge obedience to him instead.[118]

The inhabitants of some of the outlying provinces likewise tried to break away from the central authority of the state. Ṭabarī reports that when 'Alī's situation became increasingly unstable, the people of the Iranian provinces of Fars and Kirman stopped paying their land taxes (*kharāj*). 'Alī dispatched his able governor of Persia, Ziyād ibn Abīh,[119] to restore them to their former state.[120] Furthermore, the

115. Ibn Muzāḥim, p. 551.
116. See above, this chapter, the beginning of the section "Mu'āwiyah's Opposition;" also, the text associated with notes 38, 39, and 41, and the discussion preceding note 64.
117. Ibn Muzāḥim, p. 546.
118. al-Kūfī, vol. 4, p. 55; see also pp. 53–55.
119. Literally "son of his father," meaning that his father was unknown.
120. al-Ṭabarī, vol. 5, p. 137.

people of Bahrain who had recently embraced Islam reverted to their Christian faith.[121]

'Alī's authority was further eroded by his disastrous loss of the important province of Egypt along with two of his closest supporters. Soon after his accession to the caliphate, 'Alī had appointed Qays b. Sa'd b. 'Ubādah of the Anṣār as governor of Egypt. Qays was well received, as he was a peaceful, tolerant, and wise governor. However, the inhabitants of a town called Khirbittah were deeply troubled by 'Uthmān's death and asked Qays not to insist on their *bay'ah* to 'Alī until they saw what the people would decide concerning 'Uthmān's murderers. Qays consented to their demand, as he was convinced that they intended no rebellion.

Mu'āwiyah, however, feared being trapped at Ṣiffīn between the combined armies of Iraq and Egypt. He therefore forged a letter from Qays, in which Qays offered him allegiance and requested military help to avenge the blood of 'Uthmān. Mu'āwiyah then circulated this false rumor widely, so that 'Alī would come to know of it. 'Alī became suspicious of Qays's motives and ordered him to fight the people of Khirbittah. Qays, however, refused and abdicated his post. Boasting of the success of his plot, Mu'āwiyah declared before an assembly of men of the Quraysh, "I have never devised a scheme so marvellous as that with which I beguiled 'Alī against Qays."[122]

'Alī then sent Muḥammad b. Abū Bakr as governor of Egypt. In the meantime, Mu'āwiyah sent 'Amr b. al-'Āṣ, at the head of a large army including fighters of his own private police force, to secure the province. 'Amr defeated Muḥammad b. Abū Bakr and took charge of Egypt. He then had the son of his fellow Companion killed and burnt in the skin of a dead donkey.[123]

After considering restoring Qays to his old post, 'Alī decided to

121. See Wellhausen, p. 99.

122. al-Ṭabarī, vol. 4, pp. 451–452. Ibn Hilāl al-Thaqafī (pp. 127 ff.) reports that Mu'āwiyah in fact forged a letter in Qays's name wherein the latter declares his allegiance to Mu'āwiyah and asks for military help in avenging 'Uthmān's blood.

123. Ibn Khayyāṭ, vol. 1, p. 218; al-Thaqafī, pp. 185–186, and al-Ṭabarī, vol. 5, p. 105.

send Mālik al-Ashtar to deal with the thorny problem of Egypt. But Mu'āwiyah sent one of his men, who befriended al-Ashtar as he was on his way to Egypt and provided him with food and fodder for his animals. The man then treacherously killed al-Ashtar with a poisoned honey drink. In anticipation of the success of this plot, Mu'āwiyah asked the people of Syria to pray for al-Ashtar's death. Thus when the news reached him, he reassured them saying, "Do you see how your prayers were answered?"[124] The death of al-Ashtar was a devastating blow to 'Alī, for it deprived him of a faithful friend and a brave warrior.

Mu'āwiyah likewise sent military contingents to various regions in order to intimidate the people and coerce them into pledging allegiance to him. To this end, he dispatched his trusted commander Busr b. Abī Arṭa'ah al-'Āmirī at the head of a considerable force, to the region of Yaman by way of the Ḥijāz. Busr threatened and insulted the Anṣār of the Prophet's City, saying, "You company of Jews and sons of slaves, by God, I will inflict upon you such a reprisal as would comfort the hearts of the people of faith and the family of 'Uthmān. By God, I shall make of you tales like those of bygone nations."[125] Busr then forced the people of the Holy City, including its venerable governor Abū Ayyūb al-Anṣārī, to choose between death or giving *bay'ah* to Mu'āwiyah. He then dismissed Abū Ayyūb and installed the well-known *ḥadīth* transmitter, Abū Hurayrah, as governor in his place.

Busr similarly forced the people of Makkah at the point of the sword to give their *bay'ah*. Al-Mughīrah b. Shu'bah spoke to him concerning the city of al-Ṭā'if, which he spared. But Busr sought out 'Alī's supporters in the city and its surrounding areas and had them executed. Nor did he spare children, as he had two young sons of 'Ubayd Allāh b. 'Abbās, the younger brother of 'Abd Allāh Ibn 'Abbās, put to death.[126]

Busr then proceeded to the Yaman, where he secured the allegiance

124. al-Thaqafī, p. 168, also pp. 167–169; al-Ya'qūbī, vol. 2, p. 194.
125. Ibn Abī al-Ḥadīd, vol. 2, p. 10; see also pp. 3–17.
126. al-Kūfī, vol. 4, p. 59.

of its people and put to the sword all those he could find of the *shīʿah* of ʿAlī in the regions of Ṣanʿā' and Ḥaḍramawt. Finally, ʿUbayd Allāh b. ʿAbbās encountered Busr with a large Yamanite force and temporarily drove him out of the region. Busr's defeat, however, was an insignificant setback that did not deter Muʿāwiyah from pursuing his caliphal ambitions.[127]

The struggle for authority between ʿAlī and Muʿāwiyah continued as each one appointed his own *ḥajj* leader for the year A.H. 39 (660). Muʿāwiyah sent Yazīd b. Shajarah al-Rahawī, who was a pious and peaceful notable of Syria, to lead the sacred pilgrimage rites. Yazīd clashed with Qatham b. ʿAbbās, ʿAlī's governor of Makkah and hence the legitimate *ḥajj* leader. Yazīd expelled Qatham and put Shaybah b. ʿUthmān of the tribe of ʿAbd al-Dār in charge of the Holy City. In the absence of Qatham, Shaybah led the *ḥajj* for that year.

ʿAlī did not have to contend with only Muʿāwiyah. The unseemly quarrel over the leadership of the *ḥajj*, one of Islam's most solemn rites and the fifth pillar of the faith, offended Muslims in general and the Kharijites in particular. It was no doubt an important impetus to their rebellion against ʿAlī.[128]

The Kharijites based their opposition to ʿAlī on three points. The first was his consent to the deletion of the title "Commander of the Faithful" from the truce document with Muʿāwiyah. The second was his failure to strike them (the Kharijites) with the sword, "until they return[ed] to God's command," when they rebelled against him and agreed to arbitration. Their third objection was to his refusal to repent of having accepted arbitration as they did and return to God's judgment.

As for the first objection, ʿAlī argued that he had only followed the example of the Prophet in the truce of Ḥudaybiyyah. Secondly, he had

127. For a detailed discussion of the raids of Muʿāwiyah's armies against the various regions of the Muslim domains, see al-Thaqafī, pp. 288, 320, 344, and 404.

128. Ibn Khayyāṭ, vol. 1, p. 226. This was in A.H. 39, about ten months before ʿAlī's assassination. al-Kūfī's alternative report, that Ibn ʿAbbās was the *ḥajj* leader for that year, seems implausible. See al-Kūfī, vol. 4, p. 72.

not stricken them with the sword because, he continued, they were a large multitude, while he and the men of his household were few, and God said, "Cast not yourselves with your own hands into perdition" (Q.2:195). With regard to the third objection, namely his refusal to abjure arbitration, 'Alī argued that arbitration was necessary, as "God enjoined the arbitration of just men even in the case of a rabbit, worth no more than a quarter dirham."[129]

The strict, but irrational, religious logic of the first revolutionary movement in Muslim history stands out even more sharply in the following exchange between the Kharijites and 'Alī just before the battle of al-Nahrawān. This battle, which took place on 9th Ṣafar, A.H. 40 (July 17, 658), marks the beginning of Kharijite opposition not only to 'Alī's rule, but to the Qurayshite caliphate altogether. 'Alī advanced against them with a large army, but before the start of battle he faced them and cried out, "O people, I am 'Alī ibn Abī Ṭālib, speak and tell me the reasons for your indignation towards me."

The Kharijites responded with three counts on which they were angry with 'Alī. Their first point of contention was that, when they fought beside him against the people of Baṣrah in the Battle of the Camel and his fighters defeated the Baṣrans, he allowed them to pillage only what was in the enemy's camp and forbade them to take the women and children captive. 'Alī answered that the people of Baṣrah had started the fighting, thus, when he defeated them he divided the booty of those who were combatants. He did not take the women and children captive because the women did not fight and the children were born in the faith of Islam. He added that, since the Prophet pardoned the people of Makkah on the day of conquest, while they were still "Associators of other things with God" (*mushrikūn*), they should not now fault him for showing the same clemency towards Muslims.

The second point was their objection to 'Alī's having deleted his title from the Ṣiffīn truce document, as has already been observed.

129. al-Ya'qūbī, vol. 2, pp. 192–193. See for a more elaborate version of this debate, Abū al-'Abbās Muḥammad b. Yazīd al-Mubarrad, *al-Kāmil*, ed. Muḥammad Abū al-Faḍl Ibrahīm, 4 vols. (Cairo: Dār Nahḍat Miṣr, n.d.), vol. 3, pp. 11–28.

They contended, "If you are not the Commander of the Faithful, then you must be the commander of the rejecters of faith. Since we are people of faith, you cannot be our commander." Finally, they objected to 'Alī's instructions to the two arbitrators to "search the Book of God" and, in accordance with its precepts, either confirm him in the caliphate if they deemed him more worthy than Mu'āwiyah, or confirm Mu'āwiyah if they found him to be more worthy. "If," they argued, "you have doubt concerning yourself and that Mu'āwiyah may be more worthy than you, our doubt in you is even greater." 'Alī argued that he had done this in order to play fair with Mu'āwiyah, for, had he simply told the arbitrators to judge in his favor, Mu'āwiyah would not have consented. 'Alī then invoked in support of his argument the *mubāhalah* encounter between the Prophet and the Christians of Najrān, when "The Prophet did not say, 'Come let us pray and lay God's curse upon you,' but 'upon the liars'".[130]

'Alī was not able to convince all the Kharijites; he had to vanquish them on the battlefield. The Battle of al-Nahrawān not only entailed great loss of life, it transformed the Kharijites into an extremist underground revolutionary religious movement. Although this movement was finally crushed, the pattern it set continues to plague Muslim society to the present. Furthermore, the extreme and often repressive reaction the Kharijites evoked from 'Alī's Umayyad successors set a precedent for disproportionate repressive measures against any opposition to the ruling authority.

Al-Nahrawān was 'Alī's last battle. Afterward, he repeatedly tried to enlist support for a large army to crush Mu'āwiyah's rebellion once and for all, but without success. He was unable to stop even the incursions into the regions of the Islamic domains, which Mu'āwiyah carried out with increasing impunity. On his way from al-Nahrawān, 'Alī encamped in al-Nukhaylah, a suburb of Kūfah, and sent his son Ḥasan to convince the men of the city to join him in a decisive battle

130. al-Kūfī, vol. 4, pp. 122–125. For the *mubāhalah* between the Prophet and the Christians of Najrạn see above, p. 119, note 83.

against Mu'āwiyah, but to no avail. Even the men who were with him surreptitiously deserted and stole away to their homes in Kūfah. Again, al-Ash'ath b. Qays expressed well the general mood of disenchantment of 'Alī's men:

> O Commander of the Faithful, we have exhausted our arrows, and our swords and spears have become dull and useless. Return therefore with us to our city, so that we can reequip ourselves in the best manner. Perhaps the Commander of the Faithful would also see fit to add to our number the number of those of us who have perished. This would surely strengthen us against our enemy.[131]

After the Battle of the Camel, 'Alī had moved the caliphal capital, probably temporarily, from Madīnah to Kūfah, where he had strong support. Yet the Kharijite menace followed him even to this last haven. Some of the people of Kūfah sided with the Kharijites and others offered him only half-hearted support. Thus when 'Alī entered the city, a group of men of Hamadhān confronted him with the accusation, "So, you have killed the Muslims without just cause! and have trifled with God's command. You sought only kingship and allowed men to judge in the matters of the religion of God. There is no judgment except God's judgment."[132] Ibn Hilāl al-Thaqafī further reports that most of the notables of Kūfah were insincere towards 'Alī and inclined towards Mu'āwiyah. This was because 'Alī would not give anyone more than his rightful share of the state revenues (*fay'*), while Mu'āwiyah allocated an extra sum of two thousand dirhams as preferential gifts to those of noble lineage. Furthermore, 'Alī used to distribute the contents of "the house of the central treasury" (*bayt al-māl*) every Friday. Then he would sweep the floor with water in order to symbolically affirm his determination that nothing remain. He would end by performing two cycles (*rak'ahs*) of prayer and saying, "These will testify for me on the Day of Resurrection."[133] This he did in emulation of the Prophet and Abū Bakr, as he said:

131. al-Thaqafī, p. 16, and Ibn Abī al-Ḥadīd, vol. 2, pp. 193 ff.
132. al-Thaqafī, p. 20; see also pp. 16–21.
133. Ibid., pp. 30–31.

> My intimate friend (*khalīl*), the Messenger of God, never withheld any wealth for the morrow, and Abū Bakr followed his example. But 'Umar had a different opinion in that he established state registers and withheld wealth from one year to the next. As for me, I shall do what the Messenger of God did.[134]

'Alī spent the last months of his life frustrated and virtually deserted. Day after day, he would call upon the men of Kūfah to rise up against Mu'āwiyah, whose soldiers continued to intimidate the people and coerce them into pledging allegiance to him, but no one would listen. 'Alī's appeals and exhortations have been preserved in moving orations, which remain among the great gems of Arabic literature.[135] Finally, he convinced his long-time devotee Jāriyyah b. Qudāmā to resist, with a force of over two thousand horsemen, Busr's incursions against the peoples of the Yaman and the Ḥijāz.

'Alī's caliphate of under four years began in war and ended in war. He first fought the revokers (*nākithūn*) of their *bay'ah* in the Battle of the Camel. He then had to face the unjust rebels (*qāṣitūn*) at Ṣiffīn. Finally he had to wage war against the Kharijites, who have been called *al-māriqūn*, "those who slipped out of the faith," an epithet which they earned due to their disaffection from the rest of the Muslim *ummah*.[136]

The Kharijites resolved to assassinate 'Alī, Mu'āwiyah, and 'Amr b. al-'Āṣ, whose blood they considered lawful to shed. This is because the three men had, in their view, committed grave sins and thus became rejecters of faith. A group of them met in Makkah following the battle of al-Nahrawān to consider how to avenge the blood of their

134. Ibid., p. 32.

135. See Ibn Abī al-Ḥadīd, esp. vol. 2, in many places; also, al-Ya'qūbī, vol. 2, pp. 200 ff.

136. Ibn Abī al-Ḥadīd, vol. 1, p. 9; Abū Ya'la Aḥmad b. 'Alī b. al-Muthannā al-Mawṣilī, *Musnad Abī Ya'la*, 6 vols. to date (Jeddah: Dār al-Qiblah li al-Thaqafah al-Islamiyyah, 1408/1988), vol. 1, p. 269, *ḥadīth* 515; vol. 2, p. 267, *ḥadīth* 1620. See also, Jalāl al-Dīn 'Abd al-Raḥmān al-Suyūṭī, *Jami' al-aḥādīth al-masānīd wal-marāsīl*, eds. 'Abbas Aḥmad Saqr and Aḥmad 'Abd al-Jawād, 25 vols. (Beirut: Dār al-Fikr, 1414/1994), vol. 16, pt. 4, p. 238, *ḥadīth* 7796.

fellow Kharijites. They said to one another, "If we were to sell our lives to God[137] and kill the leaders of error, we would rid the earth and God's servants of them and avenge the blood of our brethren, the martyrs of al-Nahrawān"[138] They then bound themselves with a solemn oath to kill all three men on the same night, choosing the nineteenth of Ramaḍān for its special excellence.

Three men pledged themselves to carry out the plot, even at the cost of their own lives. Al-Burak b. 'Abd Allāh al-Tamīmī struck Mu'āwiyah with a poisoned sword on the buttock, but failed to kill him. Likewise, 'Amr b. Bakr, also of the tribe of Tamīm, failed to assassinate 'Amr b. al-'Āṣ. He mistakenly killed a man called Khārijah, whom 'Amr had deputed to lead the prayers that morning.

'Abd al-Raḥmān b. Muljam al-Murādī, an ally of the tribe of Kindah, along with two Kufan accomplices ambushed 'Alī as he was entering the main mosque of Kūfah to lead the morning prayers. Ibn Muljam struck 'Alī on the head with a poisoned sword. 'Alī is reported to have exclaimed as he received the fatal blow, "I have achieved my goal [that is of martyrdom] by the Lord of the Ka'bah!"[139]

Ibn Abī al-Ḥadīd reports on the authority of the well-known litterateur and historian, Abū al-Faraj al-Iṣfahānī, that al-Ash'ath b. Qays had a hand in 'Alī's assassination. He is said to have met secretly with Ibn Muljam the night before in order to finalize the fateful plot. During a sharp confrontation between 'Alī and al-Ash'ath, the latter warned 'Alī of his impending death. 'Alī is said to have angrily retorted, "Is it with death that you threaten me? By God, I care not whether I fall upon death or death falls upon me."[140]

To the end, 'Alī held fast to his principles of moral justice. Ṭabarī

137. Literally, "sell our souls," which earned the Kharijites the epithet *shurāt* (sellers). This they did in accordance with the Qur'anic verse: "There are among men those who sell their lives in quest of God's good pleasure" (Q.2:207).
138. Ibn Abī Ḥadīd, vol. 6, p. 113.
139. Mubarrad, vol. 3, p. 198. I read "*fuztu*" – "I have achieved;" an alternative, well-attested reading is "*fuzta*" – "you have achieved."
140. Ibn Abī al-Ḥadīd, vol. 6, p. 117.

reports that Ibn Muljam was brought to ʿAlī who asked him, "Have I not been good to you?" "Yes," he answered. "What made you do this?" ʿAlī asked. Ibn Muljam bitterly replied, "I sharpened my sword for forty days and prayed God that with it I would kill the most wicked of His creatures." ʿAlī said, "You shall yourself be killed with it." He then said to his son Ḥasan and those around him, "A soul for a soul; if I die, kill him as he killed me. But if I live, I will decide concerning him."[141] According to another tradition, ʿAlī is reported to have enjoined, "If I live, I shall decide; but if I die, then the decision is yours. If you choose to retaliate, then one blow for one blow; and if you pardon, that is nearer to righteousness." In fact, Ibn Muljam is said to have been killed, and his corpse burnt after his eyes were gouged with hot iron and his feet, hands, and tongue cut off.[142]

141. al-Ṭabarī, vol. 5, pp. 145 and 146.
142. al-Mubarrad, vol. 3, pp. 199–200.

7

Conclusion

It was argued at the start of this discussion that the life and career of the Prophet Muḥammad, properly speaking, belong to sacred history. Like Jesus and the early church, Muḥammad and the Muslim community lived in tumultuous times that witnessed numerous conflicts and wars. For both faith-communities it was an eschatological period, a prelude to the end of world history. Thus, like Jesus of Nazareth, Muḥammad expected "the hour"[1] of the end of the world to come during his own lifetime. Jesus declared with unshakable certainty that the people of his own generation would not die until they witnessed the "coming of the Kingdom of God."[2] With equal conviction, Muḥammad asserted that between his call to prophethood and "the hour" there was no more than the space between his two fingers.[3]

Even a cursory look at the early *sūrahs* of the Qur'ān confirms that, like the early church, the early Muslim community was an eschatological community. Hence, the eschatological worldview which dominated the Makkan as well as Madīnan periods of Muḥammad's

1. The term "*al-sā'ah*" ("the hour") is used in the Qur'ān to denote the Day of Resurrection; see for example Q.15:85, 16:77, 20:15, and 22:1, 7.
2. See Mt. 16:28, Mk. 9:1, Lk. 9:27.
3. See al-Bukharī, *Ṣaḥīḥ* (*K. al-tafsīr, bāb qawl al-nsbī*): "*bu'ithtu anā wal-sā'ah . . .*"; Muslim, *Ṣaḥīḥ* (*K. al-fitan wa ashrāṭ al-sā'ah, bāb al-sā'ah*).

prophetic career, we believe, obviated the immediate need for an independent and well-developed political and administrative system of government. This only became a necessity with the vast empire whose growth so quickly followed his death. All that the first generation of Muslims needed to do was to live by a sacred law revealed by God and instituted by His Prophet, and wait for the day of the final reckoning, which they believed to be near at hand.

It is not improbable that even in Madīnah, where he became the head of a state, Muḥammad continued to see himself not only as the last prophet, but also as the final authority of God's law on earth. Therefore, even though he may have thought one, or even several of his close companions capable of managing the affairs of the community after him, he could not in reality bequeath his Divine/Prophetic authority to anyone. Consequently, his death created a real authority vacuum that no other member of the community could fill. This perhaps explains why both the Qur'ān and *ḥadīth* tradition, in spite of all assertions to the contrary, are virtually silent with regard to the issue of succession.

We have argued above that all four "Rightly Guided" caliphs were good and pious men. The first crisis of succession was not a crisis of personalities, but of legitimate authority. The point at issue was not who, but how to choose a successor to the Prophet and clearly define the form and content of his authority. Thus we saw that Abū Bakr's *bay'ah* was opposed not on the basis of sacred tradition, but on the grounds that it lacked proper consultation. We saw also that 'Umar was himself critical of Abū Bakr's, as well as his own *bay'ah*. Furthermore, the failure of 'Umar's six-man committee to institute an acceptable method of caliphal appointment was, in our view, due to the fact that the second crisis of caliphal succession surrounding the choice between 'Alī and 'Uthmān was one of both principle and personality.

Although near kinship to the Prophet was invoked by Abū Bakr at the *saqīfah* of Banū Sā'idah as a pre-condition for caliphal authority, it did not play a significant role in this formative stage of Muslim history. 'Alī's insistence on his indisputable right to succeed the

Prophet Muḥammad as the imām of the Muslims was of little consequence in the choice of the first three caliphs. When, moreover, he did succeed in receiving the *bay'ah* of most of the Immigrants and Supporters, he did so not solely on the grounds of his close kinship to the Prophet, but also because he was the only remaining man of 'Umar's *shūra* council who was a credible candidate for the caliphate. It must in fact be concluded that neither the Companions of the Prophet nor their successors were able to arrive at a universally acceptable solution to the deep and persistent crisis of succession or caliphal appointment.

It is not till the third century of the *hijrah* that we begin to see the emergence of definite answers to the general question of authority in Muḥammad's community. These answers, however, not only aimed at defining the nature and scope of the authority of the Prophet's successors, they also provided the ideological framework of whichever sect, school or movement espoused them. They were in fact ideals, beliefs, and concepts that were either never realized, only symbolically or abstractly implemented, or simply ignored.

One of the earliest and most elaborate responses to the problem of succession was the Shī'ī doctrine of the imamate. This doctrine, however, was formulated by a persecuted minority, and over several centuries. While its ideal view of religio-temporal authority in Islam exerted much influence on Muslim, and particularly Sufi piety, the Shī'ī community had neither the strength nor the unity to implement it. Furthermore, the Shī'ī option raised the imām to the status of the Prophet, insisted on Divine/Prophetic designation (*naṣṣ*) rather than popular choice of the imām, and confined this Divine office to particular members of the Prophet's family. Because, moreover, this ideal doctrine could not be realized within the earthly life of the Muslim *ummah*, the imām, as the only true successor to the Prophet, was pushed out of world history altogether and into eschatological time.[4]

Shī'ī imamology presents not one but several answers to the problem

4. See Ayoub, *Redemptive Suffering*, chs. 2 and 6, pp. 53–68, 216–229.

of authority in the Muslim community after the death of its founder. Yet all of these answers in their doctrinal forms were too radical to be adhered to even by the imāms who did exercise authority in a Shīʿī state, such as the Fatimids of Egypt. The Twelver Imāmī or Ja'farī legal school, which has been recognized as the fifth orthodox *madhhab* on account of its well-developed juristic or *fiqh* system, evolved the most legally and theologically complete and influential doctrine of the *imāmah*, or successorship to the Prophet. Yet this doctrine remained theoretical, as it was developed gradually and outside an actual state system of authority and was, therefore, never put to the test.

It must be noted in this regard that only the first Imām, ʿAlī Ibn Abī Ṭālib, exercised authority in a Muslim state. He, however, ruled not as the imām envisioned by Shīʿī theology, theosophy, and jurisprudence, but as the *khalīfah* of the Muslims. The ten imāms who succeeded him exercised only spiritual and moral authority over their followers. As for the Twelfth Imām, he is believed to have gone into divine concealment as a child. His reappearance, moreover, will be one of the portents of the Day of Resurrection.

According to the Shīʿī doctrine of the imamate, the imām is not simply an exemplary ruler. He is also the sole possessor of the authority to interpret and implement God's law. Like the Prophet, the imām is Divinely protected (*maʿṣūm*) from error. Also like the Prophet, the imām is granted Divine favours and miracles in proof of his imamate. Furthermore, in his very existence and conduct, the imām is believed to be a manifestation of Divine grace, whose creation and appointment is therefore incumbent upon God. It is understood that God did complete His grace by creating and designating the imām. That this act of Divine grace remained inoperative in the Muslim community, the doctrine argues, is due not to God, but to the community's obstinate rejection of the imām, and hence of Divine grace.[5]

5. See ʿAllāmah Ḥillī, *Kashf al-murād fī sharḥ Tajrīd al-iʿtiqād* [commentary on the *Tajrīd* of Naṣīr al-Dīn Ṭūsī], ed. Ḥasan Ḥasanzādah al-Amulī (Qum: Mu'assasat al-Nashr al-Islāmī, 1415 [1994]), p. 362. The proof-text of this divine designation is Q.5:67.

We have dwelt at some length on the Shīʿī doctrine of the imamate for several reasons. First, it provided both the basis and criteria for the theological and legal debates over the important issue of succession, an issue that played a primary role in the rise and development of the major sects and schools of early Islam. Second, it provided both the framework and criteria for subsequent legal and theological debates concerning the spiritual/ideological and temporal/practical authority of the imām as the successor to the Prophet. Third, it provided the basis and nature of the Sufi doctrine of the *quṭb* (pole) or Perfect Man upon whom the existence and well-being of the universe is said to depend. We shall presently return to this important doctrine.

The imām is not only a manifestation of Divine grace, but of Divine justice as well. The principle of Divine justice, which implies Divine grace, is one of the five fundamentals of Muʿtazilite theology. While the Muʿtazilites did not accept the Shīʿī doctrine of the imamate, the doctrine was, nonetheless, based on Muʿtazilite principles. This is because Shīʿī theology in general is heir to Muʿtazilite rational theology. In the end, however, Muʿtazilism disappeared as a theological school and Shi'ism, as a developed legal and theological system (*madhhab*) still awaits a just and equitable state (*dawlah*) under a just imām. This hope is daily prayed for by Twelver Imāmī Shīʿīs in the words: "O God, we beseech you for a noble state in which you bestow honor on Islam and its people and humiliation on hypocrisy and its people."[6]

We argued above that Shiʿism and Sufism may be regarded as the two most important protest movements against the despotic authority, wealth, and worldliness of the rapidly expanding and powerful Muslim empire which followed the death of the Prophet Muḥammad. While the Shīʿī protest was political, and often revolutionary, that of Sufism expressed itself, at least in the formative stages of Sufi history, in an

6. This prayer is part of the ritual devotion to the Twelfth Imām, which is repeated by pious Shīʿī Muslims after every canonical prayer.

ascetic rejection of the world with all its wealth and pleasures. Hence the perfect leader or shaykh is not a good and just ruler, but an anonymous perfect man. He is an intimate friend (*walī*) of God, the grace, or blessing (*barakah*) of whose presence in the world is necessary for its well-being. The imāms likewise, are the proofs (*ḥujaj*) of God over His creation. They are the pillars or supports (*arkān*) of the earth, without whom it would quake and melt away.[7]

It should be further observed that the concept of *walāyah* (saintship or Divine/saintly authority) is common to both Shī'ī and Sufi theosophy. For both, *walāyah* is the inner dimension of prophethood. The *walī* therefore is not an ideal leader, or an imām in the narrow sense of the word, but a manifestation (*maẓhar*) of God in human form.

As Divine/human beings, neither the Sufi *quṭb* nor the Shī'ī imām could provide an actual model for a Muslim ruler, be he a traditional caliph, later sultan, or the head of a modern Muslim state. This is because the Sufi *quṭb* was never conceived as a ruler, and the imām in occultation (*ghaybah*) could not exercise direct authority in a Shī'ī, let alone Islamic state. Nonetheless, the Shī'ī insistence on the right of 'Alī and his descendants to succeed the Prophet as the imāms of the Muslims, on the one hand, and the Sunni conviction of the legitimacy of the caliphate of Abū Bakr, 'Umar, and 'Uthmān, on the other, continue to divide the Muslim community into two opposing and irreconcilable camps.

The Shī'ī ideal of a just and infallible imām of the descendants of the Prophet, and the constant struggle to realize this ideal posed a great challenge to Sunni traditionists and political theorists. It forced them, in the end, to sacrifice religious principles to political expediency and the ideal of a just ruler to social peace and order. Both Shī'ī and Sunni traditions concur on the Prophetic dictum that the imāms ought to be of the Quraysh.[8] In contrast, the Kharijites rejected

7. See Muḥammad b. Isḥaq b. Ya'qūb al-Kulaynī, *al-Uṣūl min al-kāfī* (*K. alḥujjah, bāb al-a'immah hum arkān al-arḍ*).

8. This cryptic ḥadīth reads, "*al-a'immah min quraysh*," lit. "The imāms are of the

genealogical affiliation as a pre-condition for caliphal authority altogether, insisting instead on piety and right belief. However, their ideology was repudiated by both Sunni and Shīʿī traditionists and theologians and therefore had no bearing on the development of political thought in Islam.

It was repeatedly observed in this study that to the end of his life ʿAlī insisted on his right to inherit Muḥammad's authority over the Muslim community. He passionately defended this right immediately after ʿUthmān received the *bay'ah* of the other members of the *shūrā* council and the other men present. He argued, "I adjure you by God! Is there anyone among you with whom the Messenger of God established a pact of brotherhood with himself when he made [each man of the Immigrants a brother of one of the Supporters] besides me?"[9] "No," they answered. He went on, "Is there anyone among you concerning whom the Messenger of God said, 'Anyone of whom I am master, this man is also his master,' besides me?" Again, they answered, "No." He then asked, "Is there anyone among you to whom the Messenger of God said, 'You are to me in the same station as Aaron was to Moses, except that there will be no prophet after me,' besides me?" They said, "No."[10] Thereupon, he reminded them of the time when the Prophet deputed him to convey the first verses of *sūrah* 9 (*barā'ah* – Disassociation) and declared, "No one shall convey my

Quraysh." Bukharī (*K. al-aḥkām*) and Muslim (*K. al-imārah*) substitute instead *umarā'* ("the chief"). Ibn Hanbal, in his *Musnad*, in the chapter on Anas b. Mālik (*ḥadīth* 12433) and the chapter on Abī Barzah al-Aslamī (*ḥadīths* 18941 and 18967) uses the term "*a'immah*."

9. It is reported that soon after the Prophet and the Immigrants arrived in Madīnah, he established a pact of brotherhood between each man of the Immigrants and a man of the Supporters. Left without a brother, ʿAlī sorrowfully complained, "O Messenger of God, you did not make a pact of brotherhood between me and anyone." The Prophet answered that he had kept ʿAlī for himself, to be his brother. See Muḥammad Bāqir Majlisī, *Biḥār al-anwār*, 110 vols. (Beirut: Mu'asassat al-Wafā', 1403/1983), vol. 38, p. 334.
10. This is what the Prophet is reported to have said to ʿAlī after declaring him to be his brother. Shīʿī traditionists and theologians have used this report as a proof-text for the imamate of ʿAlī. See note 9, above.

words except me or one who is nearest to me."[11] He also reminded them that, while many of the Companions had abandoned the Prophet in the face of danger, he, 'Alī, had never deserted him on the field of battle. They all assented to the truth of this. He continued, "Do you know that I was the first to accept Islam?" "Yes," they answered. "Who of the two of us ['Alī and 'Uthmān] is nearer in kinship to the Messenger of God," 'Alī asked. "You," they said. But 'Abd al-Raḥmān b. 'Awf interrupted him saying, "O 'Alī the people would have no one but 'Uthmān; do not therefore give them a cause against you." He then turned to Zayd b. Sahl al-Anṣārī, whom 'Umar had appointed to oversee the deliberations of the six men, and asked, "O Abū Ṭalḥah, what did 'Umar command you to do?" "He commanded me to kill the man who disrupts the unity of the community," Zayd replied. 'Abd al-Raḥmān turned to 'Alī and said, "Give your *bay'ah* now, or you will not be following the way of the people of faith, then we would have to execute you as we have been commanded." 'Alī finally acceded to their demands, saying, "You [all] know that I am more worthy of it [the caliphate] than anyone else, but by God, I will submit." He then put out his hand and offered his *bay'ah*.[12]

We have quoted this report extensively because, with minor variations, it has been accepted by both Shī'ī and Sunni tradition. For Shī'īs, however, the points that 'Alī used to argue his case constitute the basis of the doctrine of the imamate. Albeit they do present a good defense of 'Alī's right to the caliphate, a right he was repeatedly denied, in themselves 'Alī's arguments do not provide a framework for a theory or doctrine of succession. The actual formulation of that theory occurred over time and in response to contemporaneous events and abstract imperatives.

11. During the first *ḥajj* pilgrimage after the conquest of Makkah and a year before the Prophet's farewell pilgrimage, the beginning verses of Surah 9, disassociating God and His Prophet from any pact with the "rejecters of faith," were revealed. The Prophet first sent Abū Bakr to recite these verses to the pilgrims, but then sent 'Alī to take over as his deputy. See Abū al-Faḍl b. al-Ḥasan al-Ṭabarsī, *Majma' al-bayān fī tafsīr al-qur'ān*, 6 vols. (Beirut: Dār Maktabat al-Ḥayāt, 1380/1961), vol. 3, p. 9.
12. Ibn Abī al-Hadīd, vol. 6, p. 167.

Ṭabarī reports that before his death of the wound inflicted on him by ʿAbd al-Raḥmān b. Muljam, ʿAlī was asked, "If we lose you, and may we never lose you, should we give *bay'ah* to Ḥasan?" He answered, "I will neither command you nor forbid you, you know best."[13] It is probable, in our view, that ʿAlī was not in favor of hereditary rule, although he most likely considered himself and his family to have a special social and spiritual priority as people of the Prophet's household (*ahl al-bayt*). Yet hereditary rule, which is contrary to the Islamic concept of open consultation (*shūrā*), was legitimized by both Shīʿī and Sunni political theory and practice. It is in fact an essential element of the Shīʿī doctrine of the imamate.

ʿUmar, as we saw, refused to appoint his successor, and even more vehemently not his own son. ʿUthmān, in contrast, contemplated appointing his son as his successor, but was prevented by circumstances.[14] Whether ʿAlī actually commanded it or not, his followers pledged allegiance to his son Ḥasan. Ḥasan, however, wisely abdicated to Muʿāwiyah in order to stop further bloodshed, and lived quietly in Madīnah.[15] Muʿāwiyah was made caliph by default. He ruled the Muslim state very successfully over two decades and greatly expanded both its borders and its powers.

The appointment by a caliph of his own successor, for which Abū Bakr set a precedent that ʿUmar then repudiated, was defended by Muʿāwiyah. It is reported that soon after his accession to the caliphate, Muʿāwiyah had Ibn Ḥuṣayn, a prudent and highly intelligent man, brought to him secretly by night and queried him: "I have been told that you are a man of keen mind. I want therefore to ask you a question and I want your candid answer. Tell me what was it that disrupted the unity of the Muslims, dispersed their aims, and spread dissension among them?" Ibn Ḥuṣayn answered, "It was the murder of ʿUthmān." "You have not guessed right," Muʿāwiyah retorted. The man responded, "Then it was ʿAlī's fighting against you at Ṣiffīn." Again,

13. al-Ṭabarī, vol. 5, pp. 146–147.
14. See Madelung, pp. 88–89.
15. Ibid., pp. 330–331.

Mu'āwiyah told him that he had missed the mark. Ibn Ḥuṣayn then suggested the Battle of the Camel as the cause of Muslim disunity. But Mu'āwiyah again told him that he was wrong. The man said in desperation, "I have nothing else to say, O Commander of the Faithful!" "I will tell you," Mu'āwiyah said.

> Nothing disrupted the unity of the Muslims, dispersed their aims, and created dissension among them except the *shūrā* that 'Umar entrusted to six men. This is because God sent Muḥammad "with right guidance and the religion of truth, in order that He make it prevail over all religion, though the Associators (*mushrikūn*) may hate it" (Q.9:33; also 48:27 and 61:9). Muḥammad did as God had commanded him, until He received him up to Himself. [On his deathbed] Muḥammad brought Abū Bakr to the fore to lead the Muslims in prayer. They therefore chose him to lead them in the management of their worldly affairs, just as the Messenger of God chose him for the affairs of their religion. Abū Bakr followed the *sunnah* of the Messenger of God and walked in his footsteps until God took him. He appointed 'Umar, who followed his example. 'Umar then entrusted [the choice of his successor] to six men, each one of whom coveted the caliphate for himself and whose own people desired it for him. Had 'Umar appointed his successor as Abū Bakr did, there would have been no opposition.[16]

Mu'āwiyah, however, did not only appoint his successor; he imposed his son Yazīd as caliph after him, even though he was regarded by the majority of Muslims as being unfit for the office. After Mu'āwiyah, hereditary rule became the norm and has prevailed to the present. Furthermore, Yazīd's appointment sparked another, and much bloodier civil war than that of Ṣiffīn, and led to the ultimate demise of the Umayyad dynasty.

The purpose of this study has been to examine the interaction of religion and politics during the formative period of Muslim history. Muslim scholars have generally studied this crucial period each from his or her ideological or sectarian point of view. Western scholars have likewise taken sides with this or that party, or largely neglected the religious dimension in favor of political interpretations. We, on the

16. Ibn 'Abd Rabbih, vol. 5, p. 31.

other hand, have endeavored to give equal attention to religion and politics, but without weighting our argument in favor of any sect, ideological position, or party. This we did by always examining political events and ideas in their broad religious context. It is our hope that this study has succeeded, however modestly, in achieving this goal.

Appendix I

The Four "Rightly Guided" Caliphs in their Own Words

The orations and sermons attributed to the four "Rightly Guided" caliphs reflect their status in Muslim piety rather than what they may or may not have said. These orations are largely pietistic and wise sermons that admonish Muslims to fear God, live moral lives, and shun worldly pleasures. They also seek to emphasize the humility, piety, and upright conduct of these caliphs and their unshakable commitment to justice and clemency in managing the affairs of their subjects. The inaugural address and a sermon of Abū Bakr, as well as a series of inaugural sermons of ʿUmar are translated below.

Unlike Abū Bakr and ʿUmar, ʿUthmān did not deliver an inaugural oration, and thus made no promises of justice or fair consultation, as had his predecessors.[1] Ṭabari relates a few brief sermons, on the authority of Sayf b. ʿUmar, that present ʿUthmān as a pious and ascetic man, but say nothing about his administrative conduct. Since, however, our purpose in including such texts is to elucidate a picture of the ideal caliphate as reflected in the orations ascribed to Muḥammad's first four successors, we shall present instead some of ʿUthmān's correspondence, also reported on the authority of Sayf b. ʿUmar, that deals more directly with his view of the leaders of the Muslims and their relations to their subjects.

1. See Ibn Shabbah, p. 957–958.

We have already quoted 'Alī's brief inaugural address in which he states his conditions for accepting the *bay'ah* of the Immigrants and Supporters. We have, moreover, discussed in some detail his view of the caliphate. We shall therefore quote his last words to the members of his household and the generality of the Muslims, words that reflect 'Alī's view of the ideal Muslim in general rather than of the ideal ruler in particular.

*   *   *

Abū Bakr's Inaugural Address

O people, I am a man like you. Yet you may charge me with things that only the Messenger of God could endure. God surely preferred Muḥammad over all of humankind and protected him from all ills. As for me, I am a follower, and not an innovator. If, therefore, I act uprightly, follow me; but if I deviate from the right course, then you must set me straight. As for the Messenger of God, he passed away without anyone accusing him of any wrongdoing, not even the light strike of a whip or anything lesser than that. But as for me, I have a satan who possesses me; avoid me when he comes to me.

I will never harm you, not even your hair or flesh, as you come and go towards a term of life that has been kept secret from you. If you can spend your life till your appointed end in righteous works, then you must endeavor to do so. Yet you cannot do so except with God's help.

Compete as if in a race while your have respite, before your fixed term of life delivers you to the cessation of all actions. There are people who forget the appointed term of their life, and thus leave [the gain] of their works for others to enjoy. Beware that you be not like them. Act with utmost seriousness and vigilance in quest of your salvation! For you are chased by a determined pursuer, a fixed term, speedy indeed is its passing. Beware death, and take a lesson from your departed fathers and sons. Do not deem the living fortunate except in what you would consider the dead fortunate as well.[2]

A Prayer Sermon of Abū Bakr

O people, I have been set in authority over you, yet I am not the best of you. Therefore, if I do well, assist me, but if I do badly, then set me straight. Truthfulness is a [precious] trust and falsehood is a [despicable]

2. al-Ṭabarī, vol. 3, p. 223.

fraud. The weak among you is strong in my sight until I restore his right to him, if God wills, and the strong is weak in my eyes until I exact the right from him. Let no one of you abandon *jihād*, in the way of God, for no people abandon *jihād* but that God shall afflict them with humiliation. Nor would God spare a people from affliction if lewdness prevails among them. Obey me so long as I obey God and His Messenger, but if I disobey God and His Messenger, you are under no obligation to obey me.[3]

* * *

'Umar's Inaugural Sermons

O people, I have been set in authority over you. Yet, had it not been for my hope to be the best among you for you, the strongest over you, and the most aware of what is important in managing your affairs, I would not have accepted this trust from you. It shall be enough care and sorrow for 'Umar to wait for the day of reckoning to give an account concerning your obligatory alms [*zakāt*] – how I exact them from you and how I dispense them – and concerning the way I rule over you. How should I rule? My Lord alone is my help, for 'Umar can trust in neither power nor clever stratagem, unless God hastens to his rescue with His mercy, succour and support.

*

God, exalted be He, has set me in authority over your affairs, and I am well aware of what is most beneficial for you. I pray God to help me in my endeavor. I also pray Him to safeguard me in it as He did in other pursuits. May He inspire me to do justice in the allotment [of wealth] among you. I am a Muslim man and a feeble servant, except as God aids me. Your caliphate, with which you have charged me, will not, God willing, alter my conduct in any way. For, greatness belongs to God alone. As for the servants, they possess nothing of it. Let no one of you say that 'Umar changed since he was charged with authority [over you] . . . Any one among you who suffers wrong [at my hand], or wishes to speak words of blame to me for improper conduct, let him bring it to my attention, for I am only one of you.

*

Fear God both in secret and in public, with regard to unlawful things as well as your family honor. Give everyone his due, even if it be against you. Let not some of you prevent others from turning to me for arbitration, for

3. Ibid., vol. 2, p. 210.

there is no special pact of leniency between me and any man. Your well-being is dear to me, and your words of blame are likewise precious in my eyes.

*

The majority of you are people who dwell in God's lands. Yet, you are the people of a land that has neither cultivation nor flowing milk except for what God brings to it. Still, God has promised you many bounties. As for me, I am responsible for my trust and my conduct and I shall, if God wills, myself deal with your affairs. I will not delegate my responsibilities to anyone; but with regard to affairs that are far away, I will entrust them to honest men of good counsel for every one of you. Nor will I charge anyone with my trust but them, if God wills.

*

O people, I wish that I could be spared [on the Day of Judgment], with nothing counted for me and nothing counted against me. I pray that, whether I live among you a long or short life, I deal with you uprightly, if God wills. And that every one of the Muslims, even if he sits in his house and does not go out for the *jihād*, will receive his portion of God's wealth . . . Be upright in the use of your wealth, which God has bestowed upon you, for little wealth gained with gentleness is better than much wealth gained through violence.

*

You are [God's] stewards on the earth, overpowering its inhabitants. God has truly supported your religion, so that only two kinds of nations remain opposed to it. The first is one that is subservient to Islam and its people, paying you the pole tax [*jizyah*] while you reap the benefits of their toil and the sweat of their brows . . . The second is one that awaits day and night God's assaults and chastisements [at your hands]. God has filled their hearts with fear, so that they find no shelter to turn to, nor any escape. For, God's armies have overtaken them unaware and descended into their midst. Thus did you attain to life's comfort and much wealth through on-going conquests and the fortification of borders: by God's permission. All this you have achieved, along with good health for all – a thing this community had never before experienced – since the coming of Islam, and to God alone be all praise.[4]

* * *

4. For these sermons see ibid., vol. 4, pp. 214–218.

'Uthmān's Letters to his Governors, Army Chiefs, and Land-Tax Collectors

To his governors he wrote:

> God enjoined the imāms to be shepherds and did not command them to be tax collectors. Furthermore, the most excellent men of this community were created shepherds and not tax collectors. Your imāms are about to become tax collectors and thus to cease being shepherds. When this happens, modesty, trustworthiness and honourable conduct will cease. Surely the best conduct for you is that you look into the affairs of the Muslims, concerning their rights and their dues. Then turn to the affairs of the people of protected faiths, take what is your due from them and give them what is rightfully theirs. Finally, consider your enemies whom you overcome, treat them with clemency.

*

To his army chiefs he said:

> You are the defenders of the Muslims and their protectors. 'Umar laid down for you [rules] that are not unknown to us; rather, he did this in concord with all of us. Let it not come to me that anyone of you wishes to alter or change anything, for then God would alter your situation and substitute other people for you. Consider well your conduct. I will likewise be fully cognizant of what God has charged me with, and will fulfil it to the best of my capacity.

*

His letter to his land-tax collectors stated:

> God has indeed created the creation in truth, and thus He accepts nothing but the truth. Take what is rightfully yours and give [others] their due. Beware your trust, guard it well and be not the first to betray it, otherwise you will be accomplices [in wrongdoing] with those who may come after you. Be of good conduct. Do not oppress the orphan or any person [of another faith] who has a covenant of protection with you, for God shall be the adversary of those who oppress them.[5]

* * *

5. Ibid., vol. 4, pp. 244–245, and for his sermons, pp. 243 and 422.

'Alī's Last Will and Testament

Just before his death, and after affirming his faith in God alone and in Muḥammad as His servant and Messenger, 'Alī said:

> I charge you, Ḥasan, and all my children and members of my household, as well as all those to whom this testament will reach, with fear of God, our Lord and your Lord, and that "you do not die except as Muslims" (Q.2:132). "Hold fast to the rope of God all together and be not divided" (Q.3:103). For, I heard the Messenger of God say: "Making peace among the people is more excellent than all the rites of fasting and prayer. Surely in discord and conflict is the ruin of religion."
>
> Consider well your next-of-kin and treat them with kindness, for then will God make your final reckoning easy. In God's name, do not suffer the mouths of the orphans to dry up and smell foul from hunger. In God's name, treat well your neighbors, for they are the charge of the Messenger of God.

'Alī then commanded the Muslims to abide by the Qur'ān and observe regular prayers and keep the fast of Ramaḍān. He continued:

> In God's name, strive [in God's cause] with your wealth and lives. In God's name, give the *zakāt* alms, for that will extinguish the wrath of the Lord. In God's name, beware that the people of the household of your Prophet be not oppressed among you. In God's name, think well of the Companions of your Prophet, for he commanded [respect] for them. In God's name, be mindful of the poor and destitute, share with them your resources. In God's name, be mindful of those whom your right hands possess, for the last testament of the Messenger of God was his saying, "I charge you to be kind to the weak ones, those whom your right hands possess."

* * *

> Speak well to all people, as God has commanded you (see Q.2:83). Do not abandon enjoining the good and dissuading from evil, for otherwise this [trust] will be given to others. Then you would pray, but your prayers would not be answered.
>
> Strive for true humility, mutual assistance and fairness. Do not cut yourselves off [from your kinsfolk], cause disunity, or turn back from your commitments. "Assist one another in works of righteousness and piety, and do not assist one another in sin and transgression. Fear God, for God is severe in punishment" (Q.5:2).[6]

6. Ibn Abī al-Ḥadīd, vol. 6, pp. 120–121. See also al-Ṭabarī, vol. 5, 147–148.

Appendix II

The Ṣiffīn Truce Document

The conditions for the truce and arbitration reached at the end of the war of Ṣiffīn have been preserved in a document which has come down to us in two versions. The document has itself been the subject of much debate among both Muslim and Western scholars,[1] to the point where even its authenticity has been challenged. On the whole, Western scholars have viewed it as a purely political document reflecting tribal and geographical conflicts and special interests. Muslims scholars, on the other hand, have followed one of two approaches to this text. Sunni historians and traditionists have generally sought to incorporate it into an all-inclusive and irenic political theory aimed at legitimizing all the actions of the four "Rightly Guided" caliphs and their Successors (*al-tābiʿūn*). Shīʿīs have regarded the Ṣiffīn incident, including the truce outlined in this document, as a grievous act of treachery and wrong-doing towards the people of the household (*ahl al-bayt*) of the Prophet.

We believe that the document under consideration is of special significance both politically and theologically. This is because the truce was the culmination of a great conflict in which the clash of

1. For a close analysis of both versions, see Martin Hinds, "The Siffin Arbitration Agreement," *Journal of Semitic Studies*, 17.1 (Spring 1972); pp. 93–129; and A. F. L. Beeston, *Arabic Literature to the End of the Umayyad Period* (Cambridge, N.Y.: Cambridge University Press, 1983), pp. 142–147.

religion with political interests played a central role. Since we have already analyzed the salient features of this document, we shall offer here a translation of its text and leave our readers to draw their own conclusions.

Most classical historians and traditionists include both, or at least one, of the two versions of the document in their accounts of the conflict of Ṣiffīn.[2] It is noteworthy that Naṣr b. Muzāḥim, the earliest historian of this conflict, records both versions and briefly comments on their differences. As the two versions agree on most essential points, we shall translate in full the first version reported by him – which presents a more detailed account of the truce and arbitration conditions – and only summarize the points of difference contained in the second version.

* * *

The Document (following Naṣr b. Muzāḥim's first version)

Naṣr [b. Muzāḥim] reported on the authority of ʻUmar b. Shimr, who reported on the authority of Jābir [al-Juʻfī], who said: "I heard Zayd b. Ḥasan [b. ʻAlī] speak of the document concerning the two arbiters, to which he added certain things regarding the number of witnesses, as well as words not mentioned by Muḥammad b. ʻAlī al-Shaʻbī." Jābir is said to have dictated the document to ʻUmar from a copy that he had made of the original document. He said:

This is what ʻAlī b. Abī Ṭālib and Muʻāwiyah b. Abī Sufyān and their respective parties [*shīʻah*] agreed upon as subject to arbitration in accordance with the Book of God and the *sunnah* of His Prophet. ʻAlī's case is on behalf of his party of the people of Iraq, those of them present and those absent, and Muʻāwiyah's case is on behalf of his party of the people of Syria, be they present or absent. They said: We accept the judgment of the Qur'ān in whatever it judges, and consent to its command in whatever it commands. This alone shall unite us. We agree to make the Book of

2. al-Ṭabarī presents version 2; see vol. 5, pp. 53–55. al-Kūfī's brief account combines elements of both versions, vol. 4, pp. 14–15. al-Yaʻqūbī mentions two documents, one dictated by ʻAlī and the other by Muʻāwiyah, but does not report either of them; see vol. 2, pp. 189–190.

God, from its opening to its concluding [*sūrahs*], an arbiter between us concerning all that upon which we have differed. We agree to abide by whatever the Qur'ān has stipulated and abandon whatever it has abolished. It is on this that they have rested their cases and to it they have consented.

Furthermore, 'Alī and his party agree to delegate 'Abd Allāh b. Qays [Abū Mūsā al-Ash'arī] to act as their arbiter and deputy, while Mu'āwiyah and his party elect 'Amr b. al-'Āṣ as their arbiter and deputy. 'Alī and Mu'āwiyah, moreover, bind the two arbiters with God's covenant – the gravest of covenants with which God might bind anyone of His creatures – that they take the Qur'ān as a guide concerning the task with which they have been entrusted, and that they resort not to any other source in their judgment concerning what they find inscribed therein. As for what they do not find described in the Qur'ān, they must refer it to the uniting [*jāmi'ah*] *sunnah* of the Messenger of God. Nor will they intentionally seek to contradict in any way [the Qur'ān and *sunnah*], let themselves be swayed by their own whims and desires, or give in to false conjecture.

'Abd Allāh b. Qays and 'Amr b. al-'A¯ṣ likewise bind 'Alī and Mu'āwiyah with God's pact and strict covenant to accept their judgment, [which shall be consonant] with the Book of God and *sunnah* of His Prophet. Nor will they revoke this judgment or counter it with another decision. They [the two arbiters] stipulate further that they must be secure in regard to their blood, their property and their households, so long as they do not transgress the truth, whether it be accepted or rejected by anyone. The community shall, moreover, be their supporters in their just judgment.

If either of the two arbiters die before the conclusion of arbitration, the commander of his party and his people shall appoint another man in his stead. They shall elect a man from among the upright and just people, one who is in full accord with his predecessor in his commitment to judge in accordance with the Book of God and the *sunnah* of His Messenger. He shall as well be bound by the same conditions as his predecessor. Similarly, if either of the two commanders die before the stated term, his people shall appoint in his stead another man whose upright conduct is acceptable to them. The case shall remain valid, as will the [conditions for] negotiation between them. All arms shall be laid down and peace and truce shall prevail.

The two arbiters shall be bound by God's covenant, that they will make every effort to not intentionally commit wrongdoing or fall into error. Nor shall they transgress the judgment of the Book of God and *sunnah* of the Messenger of God. If they do so, the community will be free from any obligation to abide by their judgment. They will then have neither covenant [*'ahd*] nor protection [*dhimmah*].

The case shall stand as stipulated in this document, whose conditions shall be binding on both the two commanders and the two arbiters, as well as their respective parties. God is the nearest witness and keeper. All people, their families and possessions, shall be secure till the end of the stipulated period. Arms shall be laid down and all highways shall be made safe and free. Those who are present and those who are absent of the two parties shall be equally secure.

The two arbiters may choose to make their headquarters in a spot between and equidistant from Syria and Iraq, and only those who are acceptable to them shall openly visit them there. The Muslims have fixed the term for the two judges to render their judgment as the end of the month of Ramaḍān. They however can, if they so choose, either conclude their arbitration before the end of Ramaḍān, or extend it to the end of the *ḥajj* pilgrimage season. If the two arbiters do not arrive at a verdict consonant with the Book of God and *sunnah* of His Prophet by the end of the *ḥajj* pilgrimage season, the Muslims shall return to their former state of war, nor shall any condition between the two parties be binding.

The community shall be bound by God's covenant to abide fully by all that this document contains. They shall, moreover, be a united force against anyone who seeks to deny it, use it to commit wrongdoing, or attempt to contradict it.

The document was witnessed by three men of 'Alī's party: 'Abd Allāh Ibn 'Abbās, al-Ash'ath b. Qays, and Mālik al-Ashtar. Mu'āwiyah's witnesses were Ḥabīb b. Maslamah al-Fihrī, Abū al-A'war b. Sufyān al-Sulamī, 'Alqamah b. Ḥakīm, and Ḥamzah b. Mālik. They witnessed, saying: "Between us is God's pact and covenant that we will abide by all that is in this document." 'Umar b. Shimr wrote down the document on Wednesday, the seventeenth of Ṣafar of the year 37.[3]

*   *   *

Discussion of the Second Version

Ibn Muzāḥim designates the second version of this document as "another copy or form (*sūrah*) of the arbitration document." He reports it on the authority of Abū Ishāq al-Shaybānī, who said: "I read the truce treaty, which was with Sa'īd b. Abū Burdah [that is Abū Mūsā

3. Ibn Muzāḥim, pp. 504–508.

al-Ash'arī's grandson]. It was inscribed on a yellow sheet having two seals, one at the bottom and one at the top, belonging to Mu'āwiyah and 'Alī. In both seals was inscribed, 'Muḥammad is the Messenger of God.'"

Ibn Muzāḥim further reports that 'Alī was asked, as he was about to write the truce document between himself and the people of Syria, "Would you admit that they are people of faith, and *muslims*?" He answered, "I would not confess that Mu'āwiyah and his companions are people of faith or *muslims*, but let Mu'āwiyah write whatever he wants, and let him affirm whatever he wants concerning himself and his companions, and let him call himself and his companions whatever he wants." Thus they wrote:

> This is what 'Alī b. Abī Ṭālib and Mu'āwiyah b. Abī Sufyān brought forth for arbitration. 'Alī b. Abī Ṭālib shall represent the people of Iraq and those with him of his party of the Muslims and people of faith, and Mu'āwiyah shall represent the people of Syria and those with him of his party of the Muslims and people of faith.

As in the first version, the two parties pledged total obedience to the Qur'ān and its judgment. They continued, "If they [the two arbiters] do not find what they seek in the Book of God, they shall resort to the just and unifying, not the dividing, *sunnah* (*al-sunnah al-jāmi'ah ghayr al-mufarriqah*)." It is noteworthy that this "just and unifying *sunnah*" is not identified as "the *sunnah* of the Messenger of God," as in the first version, which may suggest that it refers to accepted Islamic practice. There is in fact precedence for this in the recourse of the founder of the Māliki legal school, Mālik b. Anas, to the "practice of the people of Madīnah" as a source of law. If this is the case, then this second version might be the authentic rendering of the Ṣiffīn truce agreement.

Another point in favor of the authenticity of this version is its insistence on calling the people of both parties *muslimīn* and *mu'minīn* (Muslims and people of faith). 'Alī's denial of these epithets to Mu'āwiyah and his people seems to reflect later Shī'ī-Sunni polemics, particularly since this denial is not part of the actual text of the document. In all other respects, the two versions are identical in their intent and to a large extent in their wording. This and the fact that Ya'qūbī mentions two documents, one drafted by 'Alī and his people and the other by Mu'āwiyah and his people,[4] leads us to the conclusion that this important document existed from the beginning in two versions, the first representing the people of Iraq and the second the people of Syria, but God knows best.[5]

4. See al-Ya'qūbī, vol. 2, pp. 189–190; and note 2 above.
5. See for the full text of the second version, Ibn Muzāḥim, pp. 509–510; also, al-Ṭabarī, vol. 5, pp. 53–55.

Bibliography

Abbot, N. *Aishah the Beloved of Mohammed*. Chicago: University of Chicago Press, 1942. [Repr. New York: Arno Press, 1973.]

'Alī, Jawād. *Al-Mufaṣṣal fī tarīkh al-'arab qabl al-islām*. 3rd edn. 10 vols. Beirut: Dār al-'ilm lil-malāyīn, 1970–1980.

al-Amīnī, 'Abd al-Ḥusayn Aḥmad. *Al-Ghadīr fī al-kitāb wa-al-sunnah wal-adab*. 4th edn. 11 vols. Beirut: Dār al-Kitāb al-'Arabī, 1397/1977.

al-'Askarī, Murtaḍā. *'Abd Allāh Ibn Saba' wa-asāṭīr ukhrā*. Baghdad: Kulliyat Uṣūl al-Dīn, 1388/1968. [*'Abdu'lāh ibn Sabā' and other Myths*. Trans. M. J. Muqaddas. Teheran: A Group of Muslim Brothers, 1978–.]

Ayoub, M., *The Qur'ān and its Interpreters*. 2 vols. Albany: State University of New York Press, 1992.

— *Redemptive Suffering in Islam: A Study of the Devotional Aspects of 'āshūrā' in Twelver Shi'ism*. The Hague: Mouton Publishers, 1978.

al-Balādhurī. *Ansāb al-ashrāf*. 6 vols. Wiesbaden: Frantis Steiner. [Publications of the German Oriental Institute, Beirut.] Vol. 2, ed. Ihsan Abbās, 1979.

Beeston, A. F. L. *Arabic Literature to the End of the Umayyad Period*. Cambridge, N.Y.: Cambridge University Press, 1983.

al-Bukhārī. *Ṣaḥīḥ al-bukhārī*.

Crone, Patricia and Martin Hinds. *God's Caliph*. London: Cambridge University Press, 1986.

Donner, Fred M. *Narratives of Islamic Origins. The Beginnings of Islamic Historical Writing*. Princeton: Darwin Press, 1998.

E.I.^{2}, The Encyclopedia of Islam. 2nd edn. Leiden: E. J. Brill, 1954–1966.

Fayyāḍ, ʻAbd Allāh. *Tārīkh al-imāmiyyah wa-aslāfihim min al-shīʻah mundh nash'at al-tashayyuʻ ḥattā Maṭlaʻ al-qarn al-rābiʻ al-hijrī*. 2nd edn. Beirut: Mu'assasat al-Aʻlamī, 1395/1975.

Guillaume, Alfred. *The Life of Muḥammad, Translation of Ibn Isaq's Sīrat Rasūl Allāh*. 2nd edn. Lahore: Oxford University Press, 1968.

al-Ḥasanī, Hāshim Maʻrūf. *Al-Intifāḍāt al-shīʻiyyah ʻabr al-tarīkh*. Beirut: Dār al-Kutub al-Shaʻbiyyah, n.d.

Ḥillī, ʻAllāmah. *Kashf al-murād fī sharḥ Tajrīd al-iʻtiqād* [commentary on the *Tajrīd* of Naṣīr al-Dīn Ṭūsī.] Ed. Ḥasan Ḥasanzādah al-Amulī. Qum: Mu'assasat al-Nashr al-Islāmī, 1415/1994.

Hinds, Martin. "The Siffin Arbitration Agreement." *Journal of Semitic Studies*, 17.1 (Spring 1972), pp. 93–129.

Ḥusayn, Ṭāhā. *Al-Fitnah al-kubrā*. 2 vols. Cairo: Dār al-Maʻārif, 1966.

Ibn ʻAbd Rabbih al-Andalusī. *Al-ʻIqd al-farīd*. 8 vols. Beirut: Dār al-Fikr, n.d.

Ibn Abī al-Ḥadīd. *Sharḥ nahj al-balāghah*. Ed. Muḥammad Abū al-Fadl Ibrahīm. 3rd edn. 20 vols. Beirut: Dār al-Fikr, 1399/1979.

Ibn al-Athīr al-Jazarī, ʻIzz al-Dīn Abū al-Ḥasan ʻAlī b. Muḥammad. *Usd al-ghābah fī maʻrifat al-ṣaḥābah*. 1st edn. 8 vols. Beirut: Dār al-kutub al-ʻilmiyyah, 1414/1996.

Ibn Ḥajar al-ʻAsqalānī, Shihāb al-Dīn Aḥmad b. ʻAlī b. Muḥammad. *Al-Iṣābah fī tamīyz al-ṣaḥābah*. 4 vols. Beirut: Dār al-Fikr, 1398/1978.

Ibn Ḥanbal. Aḥmad. *Musnad Ibn Ḥanbal*.

Ibn Kathīr, Abū al-Fidā' Ismāʻīl. *Tafsīr al-Qur'ān al-ʻaẓīm*. 2nd edn. 7 vols. Beirut: Dār al-Fikr, 1389/1970.

Ibn Khayyāṭ al-ʻUṣfurī, Khalīfah. *Ta'rīkh Khalīfah bin Khayyāṭ*. Ed. Suhayl Zakkār. 2 vols. Cairo: Wizārat al-Irshād al-Qawmī, n.d.

Ibn Muzāḥim b. Sayyār al-Minqarī, Abū al-Faḍl Naṣr. *Waqʻat Ṣiffīn*. Ed. ʻAbd al-Salām Muḥammad Hārūn. Beirut: Dār al-Jīl, n.d.

Ibn Qutaybah, ʻAbd Allāh b. Muslim (*pseudo*). *Al-Imāmah wal-siyāsah aw ta'rīkh al-khulafā'*. Ed. ʻAlī Shīrī. 2 vols. Beirut: Dār al-Aḍwā', 1410/1990.

Ibn Saʻd, Muḥammad. *Al-Ṭabaqāt al-kubrā*. 9 vols. Beirut: Dār Ṣādir, n.d.

Ibn Shabbah al-Baṣrī, Abū Zayd ʻUmar al-Namīrī. *Ta'rīkh al-madīna al-munawwarah akhbār al-madīnah al-nabawiyyah*. Ed. Muḥammad Shaltūt. 4 vols. Makkah: Dār al-Turāth, 1399/1979.

al-Jāḥiẓ, ʻUthmān b. Baḥr. *Al-Bayān wal-tabyīn*. Ed. Ḥasan Sandūbī. 3 vols. Cairo: Maṭbaʻat al-Istiqāmah, 1366/1947.

al-Kūfī, Abū Muḥammad Aḥmad b. A'tham. *Kitāb al-futūḥ*. 1st edn. 8 vols. Ḥaydarabād: Wizārat al-Ma'ārif al-Hind, n.d. [Repr. Beirut: Dār al-Nadwah al-Jadīdah, n.d.]

al-Kulaynī, Muḥammad b. Isḥaq b. Ya'qūb. *Al-Uṣūl min al-kāfī*.

Madelung, Wilferd. *The Succession to Muḥammad: A Study of the Early Caliphate*. Cambridge: Cambridge University Press, 1997.

Majlisī, Muḥammad Bāqir. *Biḥār al-anwār*. 110 vols. Beirut: Mu'asassat al-Wafā', 1403/1983.

al-Maqrīzī, 'Alī b. Aḥmad. *Kitāb al-Nizā' wa-al-takhāṣum fīmā bayn banī Umayya wa-banī Hāshim*. Leiden: E. J. Brill, 1888.

al-Mas'ūdī, 'Alī b. al-Ḥusayn. *Murūj al-dhahab wa-ma'ādin al-jawhar*. Ed. Charles Pellat. 7 vols. Beirut: Publications de l'Université Libanaise, 1966–1979. [*The Meadows of Gold*. Trans. and eds. Paul Lunde and Caroline Stone. New York: Kegan Paul International, 1989; *Les prairies d'or*. Traduction de C. A. C. Barbier de Meynard et A. Pavet de Courteille. Ed. Charles Pellat. Collections d'ouvrages orientaux, vols. 1–3. Paris: Société asiatique, 1962–1971.]

al-Mawṣilī, Abū Ya'la Aḥmad b. 'Alī b. al-Muthannā. *Musnad Abī Ya'la*. 6 vols. to date. Jeddah: Dār al-Qiblah li al-Thaqafah al-Islamiyyah, 1408/1988.

al-Mubarrad, Abū al-'Abbās Muḥammad b. Yazīd. *Al-Kāmil*. Ed. Muḥammad Abū al-Faḍl Ibrahīm. 4 vols. Cairo: Dār Nahḍat Miṣr, n.d.

Muslim. *Ṣaḥīḥ Muslim*.

Rosenthal, Erwin. *Political Thought in Medieval Islam*. Cambridge: Cambridge University Press, 1958.

Shaban, M. A. *Islamic History: A New Interpretation*. 2 vols. Cambridge: Cambridge University Press, 1971.

Shams al-Dīn, Muḥammad Mahdī. *Niẓām al-ḥukm wal-idārah fī al-islām*, 4th edn. Beirut: al-Mu'assassah al-duwaliyyah lil-dirāsah wal-nashr, 1415/1995.

— *Thawrat al-Ḥusayn: ẓurūfūhā al-ijtimā' iyyah wa-āthūruhā al-insāniyyah*. 5th edn. Beirut: Dār al-Ta'āruf, 1398/1978. [*The Rising of al-Husayn: Its Impact on the Consciousness of Muslim Society*. Trans. I. K. A. Howard. London: Muhammadi Trust of Great Britain and Northern Ireland, 1985.]

al-Suyūṭī, Jalāl al-Dīn 'Abd al-Raḥmān. *Jami' al-aḥādīth al-masānīd wal-marāsīl*. Eds. 'Abbas Aḥmad Saqr and Aḥmad 'Abd al-Jawād. 25 vols. Beirut: Dār al-Fikr, 1414/1994.

al-Ṭabarī, Muḥammad ibn Jarīr. *Ta'rīkh al-rusul wa-al-mulūk*. Ed. Muḥammad Abū al-Faḍl Ibrahīm. 4th edn. 13 vols. Cairo: Dār al-Ma'ārif, 1382/1962. [*The History of al-Ṭabarī*. Near Eastern Series. Albany: SUNY, 1985–; esp. vol. 9, trans. Ismail K. Poonawala (1990); vol. 10, trans. Fred M. Donner (1993); vol. 15, trans. R. Stephen Humphreys (1987); vol. 16, trans. Adrian Brockett (1995); and vol. 17, trans. G. R. Hawting (1996).]

al-Ṭabarsī, Abū al-Faḍl b. al-Ḥasan. *Majma' al-bayān fī tafsīr al-qur'ān*. 6 vols. Beirut: Dār Maktabat al-Ḥayāt, 1380/1961.

al-Thaqafī, Abū Isḥaq Ibrahīm b. Muḥammad b. Sa'īd b. Hilāl. *Kitāb al-ghārāt aw al-istinfār wal-ghārāt*. Ed. 'Abd al-Zahrā' al-Ḥusaynī al-Khaṭīb. Beirut: Dār al-Aḍwā', 1407/1987.

Wellhausen, Julius. *The Arab Kingdom and its Fall*. Trans. Margaret Graham Weir. Calcutta: University of Calcutta: 1927.

al-Ya'qūbī, Aḥmad b. Abū Ya'qūb b. Ja'far b. Wahb b. Wāḍiḥ. *Ta'rīkh al-Ya'qūbī*. 2 vols. Beirut: Dār Ṣādir, n.d.

al-Zubayrī, Abū 'Abd Allāh Muṣ'ab b. 'Abd Allāh b. Muṣ'ab. *Nasab Quraysh*. Ed. A. Levi Provincal. 3rd edn. Cairo: Dār al-Ma'ārif, n.d.

Index

Notes: Most subsections are listed in chronological order for ease of reference. Footnotes are not included in this index

shūrā deliberations *(continued)*
'Uthman's claim 47–9, 152
'Alī's imamate and 52
Shurḥabīl b. al-Ṣamt b. Jabalah al-Kindī 107–8, 119
Siege of 'Uthman
consequences of 80
Ibn Qutaybah's account
rebellion and letter to Ibn Abī Sarḥ 71–2
Khayyāṭ's account
'Abd Allāh's role 73–4
'Alī and five conditions 72
Sha'bān's account of causes 77–80
al-Tabarī's account
Marwān's counsel 77
motives behind assassination 75–6
Ya'qūbī's account of murderers 75
Ṣiffīn, Battle of *see* Battle of Ṣiffīn
Ṣiffīn Truce Document 162–7
Sufism 51, 149–50
Sunni tradition 150, 153
Syrian governorship *see* Mu'āwiyah b. Abī Sufyān

Ṭāhā Ḥusayn 39
Ṭāriq b. Shihāb 92–3
Ṭalḥah b. 'Abd Allāh 43, 70
'Alī's accession and 81, 85–6
Battle of the Camel 87
al-Ṭabarī, accounts of
'Ā'ishah's role, Battle of the Camel 89
'Alī's assassination 144, 153
Battle of Ṣiffīn 109
effects of truce agreement 135
Saqīfah Debate 15–17, 21–2, 24
Shī'ī doctrine of the imamate 18–19
'Uthmān's caliphate 53
Abū Dharr's criticism 60–2
assassination and causes 75–7
Tamīm tribe 117, 129
Thābit b. Shammās 28, 83
treasury *see* allotment of wealth
tribal loyalty 11, 23–5, 64–6, 110–11, 115–18
Twelver Imāmī 148

'Ubādah b. al-Ṣāmit 61
'Ubayd Allāh b. 'Abbās 135, 138
'Umar
Saqīfah Debate
declines selection for caliphate 10, 11
Abū Bakr's election 15–16
'Alī's opposition to Abū Bakr 19–20, 21
caliphate of
Abū Bakr's endorsement 29, 31
Inaugural Sermons 158–9
administration and policies 31–4
succession question 35–8, 40–2, 79
shūrā council, policy 43–5, 152
death 40
Umayya tribe 24, 48
and Hashimites 64
and Kharijites 140
Syrian holy sites and 99
during 'Uthmān's caliphate 54, 65–6
Umm Salamah (wife of Muḥammad) 90–1
'Urwah b. Udiyah 129
'Uthmān 32
'Umar's assessment of 36
'Umar's *shūrā* council 44, 47–9
caliphate
opposition to 52–3
break with tradition 50–1, 53–4
Sha'bān's interpretation 77–80
enlargement of Mosque 55
rehabilitation of al-Ḥakam 55–6
treasurer of Madīnah and 56
'Abd al-Raḥmān's reproach 57
'Ammār b. Yāsir's opposition 58
Abū Dharr's opposition 58–62
nature of, politics and principles 63–6
during Kūfan rebellion 67–8
Mu'āwiyah's role 68, 70
'Alī's reproach 69
siege and assassination
'Ā'ishah and 70–1, 79, 88–9
rebellion and letter to ibn Abī Sarḥ 71–2
consequences for caliphate 73–4, 80
event of death 74–7, 115
death, influence on
'Alī's caliphal authority 82, 113–15, 133–5
Mu'āwiyah's claims 93–4, 98–9, 100–1, 104, 105, 107–8
letters 160